Where
God's People Meet

Grover Lowell Hartman in 1959, when he assumed the position of executive director of the Indiana Council of Churches.

Where God's People Meet

A Guide to Significant Religious Places in Indiana

Joseph M. White

Photographs by Kim Charles Ferrill

Guild Press of Indiana
Carmel, Indiana

Library of Congress
Catalog Card Number
96-79138

ISBN 1-878208-57-8

Manufactured in the United States of America

Designed by Sheila Samson

In memory of Grover Lowell Hartman

Contents

List of Photographs

Cover Photograph

Saint Joseph Catholic Church, formerly in Rockville, moved to Billie Creek Village, Parke County

Preface

Celebrating the bicentennial of the United States in 1976 provided historians with an opportune moment to impress on the public the importance of understanding the American past. Several religious leaders likewise viewed the bicentennial as a time for advancing an understanding of religion's role in the nation's heritage. Accordingly, leaders drawn from Indiana's major religious faiths came together to form the Indiana Interreligious Bicentennial Commission. One way the commission used to participate in that year's bicentennial observance was to draw attention to the state's many religious landmarks. To do so, Dr. Grover Lowell Hartman, the commission's secretary as well as executive director of the Indiana Council of Churches, organized and led the first Indiana Religious Heritage Tours, one each to southern and northern parts of the state in the summer of 1976. Each three-day tour by automobile caravan included stops at historic religious places where local experts were on hand to introduce the interfaith group of visitors to the site's background.

The legacy of the Interreligious Bicentennial Commission went beyond these Indiana Religious Heritage Tours. To sustain an interest in the state's religious past that had been stimulated in that bicentennial year, those who had served on the commission and others gathered at the Interchurch Center in Indianapolis on November 5, 1976, in connection with the Indiana Historical Society's annual meeting. Some sixty persons in attendance resolved that there should be a permanent organization to keep alive an interest in Indiana's religious heritage. The outcome of their efforts was the formation of the Indiana Religious History Association (IRHA). The godfather and driving force behind the association was, of course, Dr. Hartman, a man whose vision and inexhaustible energy nurtured the organization through annual meetings and activities in subsequent years.

One activity that the IRHA carried forward was the Indiana Religious Heritage Tours conducted annually under Hartman's energetic direction. These occasions combined fellowship among people of different religious backgrounds with a rich educational experience. After Hartman's unexpected death on November 13, 1988, at Indianapolis, the IRHA board discontinued the tours. Since 1994 the tours have been revived on a smaller scale.

To continue the heritage of those religious tours by making Indiana's religious sites better known and to honor a founder and guiding force behind its formative years, the IRHA board decided that a guide to Indiana's significant religious places should be published in Grover Hartman's memory. This guide aims to include not only the places on the automobile tours to the northern and southern parts of Indiana, but also additional sites. The guide's readers would then have a large number of sites to select when exploring the state's religious past on their own.

The idea of a book dealing with the state's religious heritage seems especially appropriate as a tribute to the life and work of Grover Hartman. His background was rooted in Indiana, and his life's work of service was directed to its churches. Born August 3, 1914, near Battle Ground in northern Tippecanoe County, Hartman was raised in the tradition of the United Brethren Church at the Liberty Chapel Church, located in Tippecanoe County about halfway between Battle Ground and Brookston. He has written fondly of his own religious upbringing at this rural congregation in *A School for God's People: A History of the Sunday School Movement in Indiana*—a work that reflects his dedication to religious education.

Education in a religious context was indeed a major dimension of Grover Hartman's life. He excelled as a student and leader at Indiana Methodists' historic DePauw University, where, in 1935, he graduated with honors in history and was class valedictorian. He went on to the American University in Washington, D.C., where he earned an M.A. in 1936, and a Ph.D. in 1946. His doctoral dissertation treated the cultural evolution of Brookston, the town in southern White County, Indiana, near his home.

During years of graduate work, he taught at Sidwell Friends School in Washington and worked as staff assistant with the Federal Council of Churches in New York. He also married Annabel Jane Spangle on September 14, 1942, and in due course he and Annabel had four sons: Lowell, Worth, Elden, and Howard.

Hartman returned to Indiana in 1946, when he came to Indianapolis as director of the Social Services division of the Church Federation of Greater Indianapolis. In 1954, he was hired as director of the Council of Churches of St. Joseph County at South Bend, Indiana. Then in 1959, he became executive director of the Indiana Council of Churches, a position he held until his retirement in 1979. Among his many accomplishments in that position was to take from idea to reality the construction of the Interchurch Center in Indianapolis, completed in 1967, as headquarters for the Indiana Council of Churches and as office center for local denominational bodies and religious organizations. He also served twenty-one years on the governing board of the National Council of Churches. In 1979, he became consultant to the National Council of Churches' commission on regional and local ecumenism.

His formal occupations were not by any means the extent of his contributions. A man of many interests, Hartman was active in a variety of civic as well as religious causes. He chaired the Indianapolis UNICEF committee, and for more than twenty years chaired the Indiana Citizens Against Legalized Gambling, an activity for which he will be long remembered in state politics.

Grover Hartman's many services to the Indiana church community were recognized during his lifetime, with honorary degrees bestowed from Ball State University, Christian Theological Seminary, DePauw University, and Manchester College. Governor Matthew Welsh named him a Sagamore of the Wabash, the state's highest honor. Thus with this volume, which evokes the richness of Indiana's religious past, the Indiana Religious History Association aims to perpetuate his memory as a religious leader who in his own way made Indiana church history, and to pay tribute to his pioneering work of promoting understanding of the state's religious heritage.

$\mathcal{A}$cknowledgments

The research and writing of this guide owe a great deal to many people. I am happy to acknowledge with sincere thanks all the following persons who assisted the project. First of all, Grover Hartman himself helped by leaving notes on the sites visited in the Indiana Religious Heritage Tours. From this basic starting point another valuable resource was *Indiana: A New Historical Guide*, an immensely informative volume by the indefatigable team of Robert M. Taylor, Jr., Errol Wayne Stevens, Mary Ann Ponder, and Paul Brockman, and published in 1989 by the Indiana Historical Society. It was a constant source of useful information about Indiana's past and present. The work of scores of surveyors in the Historic Landmarks Foundation of Indiana's sites and structures surveys provided the author with a vast fund of information on individual buildings and useful direction for choosing sites.

Librarians and archivists cheerfully assisted at several places: the William Henry Smith Memorial Library of the Indiana Historical Society, the Indiana Division of the Indiana State Library, the Indianapolis-Marion County Public Library, the Archives of DePauw University and Indiana United Methodism, the Christian Theological Seminary Library, the Indiana Historical Bureau, and at scores of main branches of the county public libraries across the state. The local history rooms at the latter libraries often hold a wealth of material on Indiana history that is not available elsewhere.

Several IRHA leaders and members assisted the guide project. An advisory committee, consisting of James J. Divita, professor of history at Marian College and IRHA president, and board members, John Baughman, professor emeritus at DePauw University, and Rev. Rudolph Rehmer of West Lafayette provided a steady stream of suggestions, information, and advice, and they reviewed successive drafts of the guide. L. C. Rudolph, emeritus librarian of the Lilly Library, Indiana University, and author of *Hoosier Faiths: A History of Indiana's Churches and Religious Groups* (Bloomington and Indianapolis: Indiana University Press, 1995) placed the results of his vast research in Indiana's religious development at the author's disposal prior to his book's publication, cheerfully offered suggestions, and reviewed the manuscript. Burdellis Carter, IRHA treasurer, administered the project's financial aspects. IRHA board member, Bruce L. Johnson, director of the Indiana Historical Society's William Henry Smith Memorial Library, drafted the successful grant proposals and edited the final text.

The guide's text is enriched with the photographs of Kim Charles Ferrill, the Indiana Historical Society's photographer, who, with the assistance of Stephen J. Fletcher, curator of visual collections of the Society's Smith Library, traveled the length and breadth of Indiana to photograph buildings pictured in the guide. The Historical Society generously donated their services for that purpose. Ferrill's substantial collection of photographs of religious buildings—only a small portion of which appears here—now enriches the Historical Society's general photographic collections.

The Lilly Endowment Inc., at whose headquarters Grover Hartman is fondly remembered, made the guide project possible through grants. The IRHA gratefully acknowledges officials of the endowment's religion division, Craig Dykstra, James P. Wind, and Edward L. Queen II, for their encouragement and support.

Introduction

From the house of worship at the reconstructed Indian village at Angel Mounds State Park near Evansville, to the Catholic sites at Vincennes that call to mind the eighteenth-century French religious experience, and then to the state's earliest Protestant congregations founded in Clark County, Indiana abounds with historic religious sites. Their presence underscores the past reality that those settling in Indiana believed in the importance of religion in daily life and the life of the local community and acted on those beliefs by establishing religious institutions.

Historic religious sites, as represented either by markers or early buildings, do not exhaust the vast and diverse treasure of the state's religious heritage found in buildings, especially those of individual congregations. Houses of worship blanket the state and serve as reminders of religion's continuing role in Indiana history and in the life of countless local communities. From the state's formative years onward, Hoosiers' local religious institutions represent a vast ongoing social history that is carried on today by at least ten thousand active congregations representing a range of religious traditions.

To highlight Indiana's heritage of religious places possessing historic, architectural, and social significance, this guide identifies and locates over twelve hundred such sites with a brief statement of information. The guide strives to serve the student of Indiana's religious traditions, those interested in the state's architectural history, and the growing number of people interested in local history. While all parts of the state have been included in the compilation, it is not intended to be an exhaustive list of every significant religious site or building, but, rather a beginning of an ongoing effort to come to terms with the state's religious heritage by means of a guide.

SELECTING RELIGIOUS SITES

How does one go about selecting historic sites and important buildings for a guide? Very carefully, it might be answered, because the pitfalls are many. One person's important site may not seem significant to another. Finding historic religious sites is not always easy because places where an initial founding was made or a first building was located are not always marked. Denominations normally point with pride to a few locations from their own tradition, but many important sites have not been appropriately marked or can even now be precisely located.

Evaluating the merits of thousands of religious buildings for inclusion in a guide is a more complex matter. Not all old congregations produced buildings of historic or architectural significance. Congregational beginnings are often modest and their physical remains transitory. For instance, from the first half of the nineteenth century, a relatively small number of religious buildings are still standing. Few historic congregations preserved old buildings as they grew with their communities. It is in the nature of a developing congregation that the early and usually modest house of worship is superseded by a more substantial one, and perhaps later with an even more elaborate structure. For the congregations listed in the following guide whose foundings date from the nineteenth century, most are now occupying a second, third, or even a fourth house of worship. Another challenge to compiling a list is that some very historic congregations have built modern buildings at new locations in recent years. These structures no longer evoke the religious experience associated with earlier buildings or preserve the material culture from the congregation's long history.

In identifying the state's buildings of historic and architectural merit, the Historic Landmarks Foundation of Indiana, in cooperation with the Indiana Department of Natural Resources' Division of Historic Preservation and Archaeology provided guidance through its Indiana Historic Sites and Structures Inventory of buildings constructed before 1940. For about fifty-seven of the state's ninety-two counties an *Interim Report* has been published listing and classifying these historic buildings. This ambitious survey rated these buildings as **Outstanding**, **Notable**, and **Contributing** in relationship to the surrounding environment. For the purposes of this guide, the religious sites with the **Outstanding** rating are designated with a star (★). These structures are **Outstanding** for their architectural or historic significance. Some are already listed on the National Register of Historic Places (NRHP), or, in the judgment of the surveyors, if they are not listed, are worthy of inclusion on the National Register. Buildings already listed on the National Register are designated with **NRHP**.

A limited number of religious buildings with **Notable** and **Contributing** ratings have been included because of their historical importance. Likewise some architecturally significant religious buildings constructed after 1940 and therefore not appearing in the Historic Landmarks Foundation surveys have been listed.

For those counties without published interim reports, sites were selected after on-site inspections of the counties. The standards of the Historic Sites and Structures Inventory were adapted to identify outstanding religious buildings in those counties, though some buildings worthy of inclusion may have been unintentionally overlooked.

A major national effort to identify architecturally significant buildings has been the Historic American Building Survey (HABS) conducted in Indiana since the 1930s. The architectural importance of these buildings is normally reinforced with historic significance. The buildings from this survey are designated with **HABS** or **HABSI**.

The United States Department of the Interior also designates National Historic Landmarks (NHL) throughout the country. The Indiana sites having a religious significance are designated with **NHL**.

Sites or institutions having extraordinary architectural or historical importance, such as all HABS sites and others, are designated **MUST SEE** (🏛), usually with a longer statement of background information.

In recognition of the Guide's origins in Grover Hartman's Indiana Religious Heritage Tours, sites on his Southern Tour are designated with **ST,** and those on the Northern Tour with **NT**.

Other sites include accredited institutions of higher learning with a religious affiliation or background, principal headquarters of Catholic men's and women's religious orders, national or international offices of Protestant denominations or religious organizations, and sites that interested individuals have nominated.

Likewise appearing are historical markers designating an important site and describing its significance or that of the building that once stood there. The guide does not include historic places or sites that lack a marker or building to focus attention on that place's past importance.

DISTRIBUTION OF SITES

The criteria for selection do not allow for listing sites of religious bodies in proportion to their current numerical strength. Given the emphasis on historic sites and older church buildings, those religious bodies with a substantial presence in the state from the nineteenth century onwards will loom large in the guide. Large and historic religious bodies inevitably have a large number of sites. The Methodist and Catholic churches have historically been the state's largest religious bodies and thus have the greatest number of entries. Other groups have fewer sites in proportion to their size in the state. Religious bodies that have developed a substantial presence only in the past half century or use modest or functional buildings lacking architectural or historic merit generally have few entries.

Though sites and structures are listed from all parts of the state, they are not necessarily distributed evenly. Hoosiers settled the state generally from south to north, hence, some of the most important historic sites are in the southern part of the state, and the counties bordering the Ohio River have some of the finest historic buildings.

RELIGIOUS TRADITIONS

In listing a building that is or has been the home of a congregation, its current name is generally given. If a church building had previously belonged to another religious tradition, then that tradition is named, if it is known. Some buildings have changed hands from one religious tradition to another, while other buildings remain with the founding tradition which itself has undergone changes of name. The reader will also find that some historic church structures have been put to secular uses such as museums, offices, or stores.

Protestant churches comprise a substantial number of entries, and the United Methodist Church, the state's largest Protestant body, has the most. It should be noted that today's United Methodist Church is the result of a series of mergers of the Methodist Episcopal Church, Methodist Protestant Church, and the Evangelical United Brethren, which had earlier resulted from the merger of the Evangelical Association and the United Brethren Church. Blacks adhering to the Methodist tradition often belonged to the African Methodist Episcopal Church, which had numerous congregations in nineteenth-century Indiana, or one of the other black Methodist denominations such as African Methodist Episcopal Zion Church or Christian Methodist Episcopal Church.

Baptists come in several varieties. The large group of churches now belonging to the American Baptist Convention can be found throughout the state from the nineteenth century onward. The Southern Baptist Convention has actively spread throughout the state only since the 1940s and thus accounts for few historic buildings. Other Baptist traditions can also be found, especially General Baptists in southwestern Indiana and black Baptists in major cities.

Another denomination resulting from mergers is the United Church of Christ that is formed primarily from churches of the Reformed tradition of Protestantism. The United Church of Christ includes the Congregational churches, with their background in New England Puritanism, and the German Protestant traditions represented in the Evangelical Church and the Reformed Church. The mainstream Presbyterian Church of today includes most of the historic psalm-singing Scottish bodies (Covenanters and Seceders) as well as Cumberland Presbyterians.

A few church buildings in rural areas were built and maintained by several congregations of different Protestant denominations sharing the same building often designated as a "union" church. These churches have no denomination named in their titles.

In addition to Christian sites, major Jewish congregations are listed, along with several sites representing Native American, Islamic, and Buddhist religions. However, fraternal organizations such as Masons, whose buildings often evoke a sense of the sacred by adapting religious architecture, are not included. Each county is introduced with a statement describing its major religious bodies. This information is drawn from the Glenmary Research Center's *Churches and Church Membership in the United States 1990* (Atlanta, 1992) that lists figures of church membership by each state and county. Since some religious bodies do not collect and report their membership figures, the religious bodies listed in the introductory statement are those of reporting churches. Their inclusion is intended to suggest in a general way the county's religious composition by mentioning at least three major groups. The reader should know that non-reporting groups such as Pentecostal or independent congregations may be as large in some counties as the groups mentioned.

Notes On Architectural Terms

Protestant Christianity is noted for the "revival." The idea of revival, however, is also found in architecture. In the guide's brief description of a religious building, its architectural style is noted, and many styles represent a "revival" of some kind. Whether a revival style or not, here are some of the most common architectural terms found in the entries:

Greek Revival—This style was introduced to the United States in the early nineteenth century and is associated with the architect Henry Benjamin Latrobe. It gained popularity throughout the country as Americans associated their political life with the democratic ideals of the Greek city-state. The style is marked by a gable front in simple wood buildings—the gable front and usually "carpenter built" stated in the entries. In more elaborate structures, it is distinguished by porticoes, columns, pilasters, pediments, and large cornices. The style was often used for Indiana churches through the 1860s.

Gothic Revival—Nineteenth-century Romantic movements in Europe rediscovered the Middle Ages and its architectural forms. The distinguishing mark of Gothic Revival is the pointed arch that is adapted to a building's exterior structure and to windows, doors, porches, roofs, and ornamentation. It gained popularity by the 1840s, and Gothic forms in various adaptations were the most prevalent style in Indiana church architecture well into the twentieth century. Because Gothic arches pointed heavenward, many regarded it as the ideal style for church buildings.

Romanesque Revival—Another popular architectural style gaining influence in the second half of the nineteenth century adapted Roman medieval forms with the use of the rounded arch, whether in a structure's overall design and in such details as windows, porticoes, door casings, and ornamentation. This style, too, was adapted in various ways well into the twentieth century.

Italianate—This style originated in Renaissance Italy and gained popularity in the United States after the Civil War. Though it was easily adapted to residences and public buildings, some examples of Italianate churches can be found in Indiana. The style is marked by large projecting eaves, tall ornate windows, and square bell towers.

Neo-Classical Revival—In the early twentieth century, classical forms reemerged in American architecture for public, commercial, and church buildings. These buildings were much larger than the Greek Revival buildings of the early nineteenth century. The Neo-Classical churches were often massive boxlike structures with such classical details as columns, porticoes, pilasters, keystones, and pedimented window and door openings.

Twentieth Century Revivals—Other revival styles include Gothic and Romanesque, which were adapted for the construction of larger churches often in urban settings in the early twentieth century. These large square structures sometimes were built right up to a street corner and employed the Gothic or Romanesque windows and decorations that echo the earlier styles.

Occasionally other styles are designated for church buildings. Jacobean or Elizabethan styles of English Gothic, echoing the late fifteenth or early sixteenth centuries, are sometimes described as "Jacobethan." Mission style suggests stuccoed walls and tile roofs. Italian or Renaissance styles suggest a variety of models in the classical tradition. Queen Anne style represents a profusion of wood ornamentation and use of wooden shingles on exterior walls. The Arts and Crafts style was used in the early twentieth century with its artfully combined use of wood and brick, usually used for smaller church structures. By the 1930s, Neo-Georgian or Neo-Colonial influences began to attract interest in church building in order to evoke a sense of the early American religious past. This style gained even greater popularity in the 1950s.

Abbreviations and Symbols

🏛	**Must See:** Site is of extraordinary historical or architectural merit.
★	Site has an **Outstanding** rating in the Sites and Structures Inventory of the Historic Landmarks Foundation of Indiana for those counties surveyed. Outstanding rating indicates the site is worthy of listing on the National Register of Historic Places.
NRHP	Site is listed on the National Register of Historic Places.
HABS	Site is listed on the Historic American Building Survey site for its historic and architectural significance.
NHL	Site is a National Historic Landmark.
ACFW	Site has been given an Allen County Fort Wayne Historical Society marker.
ST	Site was on the **Southern Tour** of the original Indiana Religious Heritage Tours conducted by Grover Hartman.
NT	Site was on Hartman's **Northern Tour**.
CR	County Road.
SR	State Road.

INDIANA REGIONS and COUNTIES

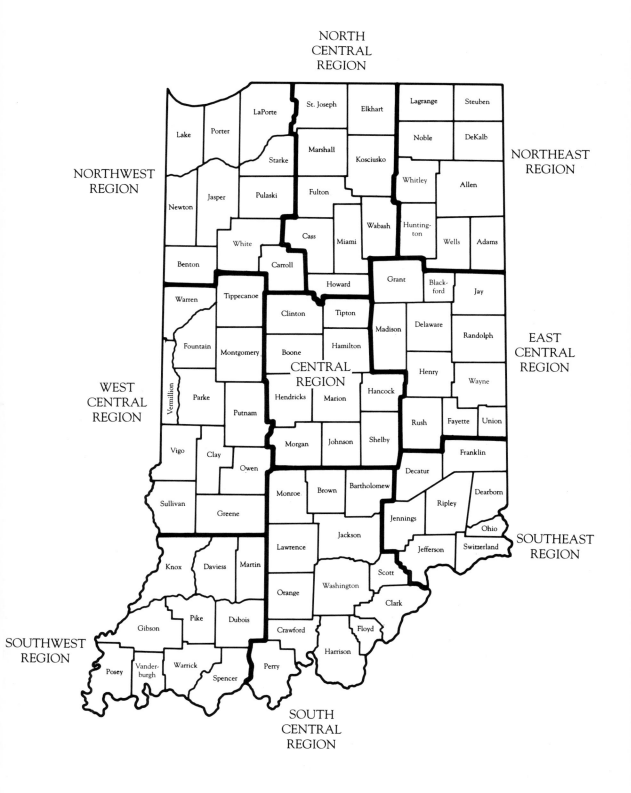

South Central Region

BARTHOLOMEW COUNTY

Bartholomew County's religious past is reflected in today's leading church groups: Christian Church or Church of Christ, United Methodist Church, and the Lutheran Church—Missouri Synod. The county seat, Columbus, is noted for its Columbus Historic District (HABS) and has won recognition for the distinguished architecture of its major modern buildings. Several of these historic and modern churches have contributed to this distinction:

🏛 ★ FIRST CHRISTIAN CHURCH, Fifth Street between Lafayette and Franklin. Organized in 1852, it was the first of Columbus's congregations to seek a world class architect by engaging Eliel Saarinen to design this striking modern church building constructed in 1940.

🏛 NORTH CHRISTIAN CHURCH, 850 Tipton Lane, near U.S. 31, is a splendid building of modern design with steeple visible for miles. The structure was built in 1964 according to design of Eero Saarinen, son of First Christian's architect; congregation was organized in 1956.

🏛 FIRST BAPTIST CHURCH, 3300 Fairlawn Drive, with unique modern design in red brick recalls medieval Gothic forms and was built in 1965 according to design of architect Harry Weese. Congregation was organized in 1852.

🏛 ★ ST. PETER LUTHERAN CHURCH, Fifth and Pearl streets, congregation organized in 1858, its red brick Gothic Revival church dates from 1903. In 1988 the congregation built a much larger church in an imaginative circular design conceived by architect Gunnar Birkerts.

★ FIRST UNITED PRESBYTERIAN CHURCH, Second and Franklin streets, a fine red brick Gothic Revival building dating from 1871–1875, congregation organized in 1824.

★ UNITARIAN-UNIVERSALIST FELLOWSHIP, Eighth between Franklin and Washington streets, formerly St. Paul Episcopal Church, a white frame Gothic Revival structure built in 1876.

★ ST. BARTHOLOMEW CATHOLIC CHURCH, Eighth and Sycamore streets, parish dates from 1841, red brick Gothic Revival building constructed in 1891.

FIRST UNITED METHODIST CHURCH, Lafayette Avenue and Eighth Street, a spacious red brick Neo-Classical building dating from 1886, congregation organized in 1823.

North Christian Church, Columbus, Bartholomew County

★ GRACE BAPTIST CHURCH, 2162 Ohio Ave, frame Gothic Revival church built for East Columbus Methodist Episcopal Church in 1910.

ELSEWHERE IN BARTHOLOMEW COUNTY:

★ MORAVIAN CHURCH, Main (SR 9) and Seminary streets, Hope, Haw Creek Township, red brick Gothic Revival building dating from 1875 with parsonage. One of the state's three Moravian congregations, the Hope church was organized in 1830 under leadership of Moravian pioneer missionary, Rev. Martin Hauser.

★ HOPE UNITED METHODIST CHURCH, Washington Street near Harrison, Hope, Haw Creek Township, brick Victorian Gothic building dates from 1887, congregation was established in 1854.

★ FIRST BAPTIST CHURCH, Jackson Street near Harrison, Hope, Haw Creek Township, brick Victorian Gothic building dates from 1888.

★ NEW HOPE CHRISTIAN CHURCH, U.S. 31, north of Columbus, German Township, stick style built in 1871 for original Christian church in county formed in 1829.

★ FAITH CHAPEL, Marr Road at CR 700N, Flat Rock Township, founded as United or Owen's Church, built in Greek Revival style around 1850.

★ TAYLORSVILLE UNITED METHODIST CHURCH, Tannehill Road (CR 650N) and East Street, Taylorsville, German Township, brick Victorian Gothic structure built in 1908, congregation dates from 1833.

★ SANDCREEK-AZALIA FRIENDS MEETING HOUSE, CR 350E and 800S, Azalia, Sand Creek Township, a fine red brick Greek Revival building dates from 1875, year of congregation's founding.

★ ST. PAUL LUTHERAN CHURCH, Market and Mill streets, Jonesville, Wayne Township, red brick Gothic Revival building dating from 1893, congregation organized in 1870.

★ OGILVILLE UNITED METHODIST CHURCH, SR 58 near CR 550S, Ogilville, Ohio Township, carpenter built structure dates from 1904, congregation dates from 1892. Historic cemetery is nearby.

ST. JOHN'S LUTHERAN CHURCH, White Creek, CR 950S and 300W, Wayne Township, red brick Gothic Revival church built in 1862 for the county's first Lutheran congregation formed by German immigrants in 1840.

ST. PAUL LUTHERAN CHURCH, SR 7 and CR 300E near U.S. 31, Columbus Township, congregation organized in 1848, present brick Victorian Gothic church dates from 1887.

Moravian Church, Hope, Bartholomew County

ST. PETER LUTHERAN CHURCH, CR 930S near SR 58, Waymansville, Jackson Township, excellent red brick Gothic Revival building dates from 1880.

CAMP LAKEVIEW, 13500 W. Lake Road, Jackson Township, is associated with the Lutheran Church—Missouri Synod. Modern camp buildings of functional design are sited on spacious grounds located on scenic Lutheran Lake.

HARTSVILLE, Haw Creek Township, site of HARTSVILLE COLLEGE, a United Brethren school, where Bishop Milton Wright, father of aviation pioneers Orville and Wilbur Wright, taught. Founded in 1850, the college was moved in 1898 to Huntington, Huntington County, and renamed Huntington College.

BROWN COUNTY

Scenic Brown County with the state's largest state park is one of the most visited spots in Indiana. T. C. Steele State Historical Site (NRHP) is a leading attraction related to the area's rich artistic tradition. The county's leading religious groups are Catholic, United Methodist, and Christian Church or Church of Christ. Nashville, Washington Township, the county seat and tourist mecca, is location of the following noteworthy churches:

★ NASHVILLE CHRISTIAN CHURCH, S. Van Buren Street (SR 135), graceful Christopher Wren-style structure built in 1932 for congregation dating from 1888.

NASHVILLE UNITED METHODIST CHURCH, W. Main and S. Jefferson streets, congregation organized in 1837, the white carpenter built Gothic Revival building was constructed in 1910 for Presbyterian Church, acquired by Methodist congregation in 1926.

ST. AGNES CATHOLIC CHURCH, SR 135 northside of Nashville, a picturesque building constructed of logs and other native materials in 1940, year of the congregation's founding.

ELSEWHERE IN BROWN COUNTY:

★ GRANDVIEW CHURCH, Grandview Road near John Butler Road, Van Buren Township, a simple gable-front structure dating from 1892 with historic cemetery, located on ridge with a "grand view." NRHP

PLEASANT VALLEY COMMUNITY CHURCH, SR 46 near SR 135 west of Gnaw Bone, Washington Township, founded as Separate Baptist congregation in 1867, a community church since late 1980s, white gable-front building dates from late nineteenth century.

COTTONWOOD CHRISTIAN CHURCH, Lick Creek Road, Cornelius, (two miles north of Helmsburg), Jackson Township, a fine, frame gable-front structure dating from 1892.

CHRISTIANSBURG UNITED METHODIST CHURCH, near SR 35, Christiansburg, Van Buren Township, congregation organized in 1866, white gable-front church erected in 1890.

CLARK COUNTY

Clark County originated with the land grant to General George Rogers Clark and his men for their services in winning the West from the British in the American Revolution. Clarksville, chartered in 1783, is the first American settlement in the Northwest Territory and hence in Indiana. In addition to historic significance Clark County attracts visitors to the Falls of the Ohio State Park. Home to some of the oldest Protestant congregations in the state, the current leading religious groups in the county are Catholic, Southern Baptist, and United Methodist.

Jeffersonville, located on the Ohio River, is the county seat. It is also the home of the Howard Steamboat Museum (NRHP), which recalls the area's shipbuilding history. The city is also home to the following historic congregations:

★ ST. LUKE UNITED CHURCH OF CHRIST, Maple and Walnut streets, founded as a German Reformed congregation in 1860, the red brick Gothic Revival building dates from 1915.

★ SEVENTH DAY ADVENTIST CHURCH, Maple and Watt streets, formerly property of a German Methodist congregation founded in 1845, which built the present red brick Gothic Revival church in 1877.

★ ST. AUGUSTINE CATHOLIC CHURCH, Chestnut and Locust streets, the present imposing Mission style church dates from 1905, parish formed in 1851.

★ FIRST PRESBYTERIAN CHURCH, Chestnut and Walnut streets, congregation formed in 1830, present red brick Gothic Revival church dates from 1860.

★ ST. PAUL EPISCOPAL CHURCH, Market and Walnut streets, parish founded in 1836, the fine Gothic Revival church was constructed in 1892.

Former FIRST CHRISTIAN CHURCH, Market and Walnut streets, opposite First Presbyterian Church, recently occupied by several church organizations; the First Christian congregation was formed in 1830 and built the present church in 1884.

BRANHAM TABERNACLE, Eighth and Penn streets, red brick functional building dates from 1933. The congregation was associated with world-renowned Pentecostal healing evangelist, William Marrion Branham, and head of Spoken Word Publications, which produced hymnals and religious literature with international circulation.

OTHER SITES IN CLARK COUNTY:

🏛 ★ SILVER CREEK BAPTIST CHURCH, Brick Church Road near Weber Road, Speed, Charlestown Township, founded in 1798 as the first Protestant and first Baptist congregation in the state. After meeting in members' homes, the first church was built in 1824. The present red brick church building in Greek Revival style dates from 1861. The building, nicely situated in an historic cemetery, is not in regular use as a place of worship. ST

★ STONY POINT CHRISTIAN CHURCH, Stony Point Road 1.8 miles north of SR 403, Charlestown Township, was formed in 1829 because of a secession of members from Silver Creek Baptist Church. The present excellent white frame Greek Revival Building dates from 1858.

SITE OF OLD BETHEL METHODIST CHURCH, about one and a half miles east of SR 160 on Jack Teeple Road, northeast of Charlestown, Charlestown Township, is designated with marker and small cemetery located about a quarter mile east of the road. The site, accessible only by crossing privately held property, is the former location of Indiana's oldest Methodist church built in 1807 by Nathan Robertson and family for congregation formed in 1801. This "Old Bethel" log chapel was relocated in 1953 to DePauw University, Greencastle, and restored. (See West Central Region—Putnam County)

OLD SALEM UNITED METHODIST CHURCH, Salem Church Road, one mile west of SR 62, Charlestown Township, founded in 1801, the present simple, small gable-front building dates from 1864 and several times remodeled.

★ FIRST UNITED METHODIST CHURCH, Main Cross Street between Water and Thompson streets, Charlestown, Charlestown Township, congregation was formed in 1801. The present Greek Revival church was dedicated in 1854. Illinois Conference (which included Indiana) of Methodist Episcopal Church was organized at Charlestown in 1825.

★ MAIN CROSS INDEPENDENT BAPTIST CHURCH, Main Cross and Pike streets, Charlestown. This former First Presbyterian Church was organized in 1812, the present red brick Gothic Revival church dates from 1877.

★ MT. LEBANON PRESBYTERIAN CHURCH, Mt. Lebanon Road at Dunley Road, Monroe Township, finely maintained white frame Greek Revival building dates from 1871, congregation organized in 1853.

★ HENRYVILLE UNITED METHODIST CHURCH, Main and Church streets, Henryville, Monroe Township, Gothic Revival church built in 1932, congregation dates from 1828.

★ ST. JOHN THE BAPTIST CATHOLIC CHURCH, St. John and Starlight roads, Starlight,

Silver Creek Baptist Church, Charlestown Township, Clark County

Wood Township, red brick Gothic Revival church built in 1913–1914, parish founded in 1861.

★ NEW CHAPEL UNITED METHODIST CHURCH, New Chapel Road at Lentzier Trace, Utica Township, finely kept red brick Gothic Revival church dating from 1883, congregation was formed in 1801 along with Salem and Old Bethel Methodist congregations.

★ UTICA CHURCH OF CHRIST, 4th and Ash streets, Utica, Utica Township, Gothic Revival structure built in 1877.

PISGAH CHURCH AND CEMETERY, Gill Road, Bethlehem and Washington Townships line, east of Nabb, is the site of one of the state's earliest Presbyterian congregations dating from early nineteenth century. It has been designated an official American Presbyterian/Reformed Historical Site.

★ ST. JOSEPH CATHOLIC CHURCH, St. Joe Road near SR 60, Silver Creek Township, red brick Romanesque Revival structure built in 1881, congregation established in 1853.

★ SELLERSBURG UNITED METHODIST CHURCH, N. New Albany Street, Sellersburg, Silver Creek Township, twentieth-century Gothic Revival church constructed in 1924–1925, congregation organized in 1871.

CRAWFORD COUNTY

Crawford County, with much of its area within the Hoosier National Forest, is noted for beautiful scenery and draws visitors to Wyandotte and Marengo Caves. Its modest population has not developed numerous religious buildings. The county's leading religious bodies are Christian Church or Church of Christ, United Methodist, and Wesleyan. This distinctive church is noteworthy:

COMMUNITY PRESBYTERIAN CHURCH, Townsend Drive near Old SR 62, Leavenworth, Jennings Township, is the town's main house of worship dating from 1937, built in a red brick Neo-Classical style. Located in the upper part of town, the church was built after the lower town's Methodist and Presbyterian churches were ruined in the Ohio River flood of 1937.

FLOYD COUNTY

Floyd County, on the Ohio River, began settlement early in the nineteenth century along with adjacent Clark County. The leading religious groups today are Catholic, Southern Baptist, and United Methodist. New Albany, the county seat, rose to prominence because of its river location to become one of the state's largest cities by the 1850s. William S. Culbertson Mansion, a state historic site, located in the Mansion Row Historic District, attests to the city's early wealth and influence. New Albany's former prominence is reflected in these historic congregations:

★ ST. JOHN UNITED PRESBYTERIAN CHURCH, Thirteenth and Elm streets, the city's first congregation dates from 1817; the present St. John congregation is the result of mergers after earlier congregational divisions. The former Second Presbyterian Church members built this imposing and elegant red brick Romanesque Revival building in 1900.

ST. PAUL EPISCOPAL CHURCH, Eleventh Street between Market and Main streets, limestone Gothic Revival church built in 1895, parish was started in 1836.

BETHEL AFRICAN METHODIST EPISCOPAL CHURCH, E. Fifth between E. Market and E. Spring streets; the local German Methodist congregation built this red brick church in Greek Revival style in 1864. Bethel AME congregation was organized in 1859.

SEVENTH-DAY ADVENTIST CHURCH, E. Spring and E. Fifth streets, was the German Methodist congregation's next church building after using the church cited above; this red brick Gothic Revival building dates from 1889.

★ SECOND BAPTIST CHURCH, or the Town Clock Church, E. Main and E. Third streets, was built between 1849 and 1852 in a beautiful Greek Revival style for the former Second Presbyterian congregation. A historical marker describes the church as a station on the Underground Railroad; its basement rooms served as a stop for fugitive slaves. In 1889 it was sold to black Baptists. Second Baptist's beautiful clock tower was a landmark for river pilots on the Ohio.

ST. MARY CATHOLIC CHURCH, Spring Street between E. Seventh and Eighth streets, was formed for the city's German Catholic immigrants in 1855 and built in Romanesque Revival style with a "Zwiebelturm" or onion-shaped spire similar to church spires in southern Germany.

HOLY TRINITY HERITAGE COURT, E. Seventh and E. Market streets, is a small park with a marker and foundation of Holy Trinity Catholic Church, built in 1852 and destroyed by fire in 1975. Holy Trinity was the city's first Catholic congregation formed in 1837.

CENTENARY UNITED METHODIST CHURCH, E. Spring between Fourth and Fifth streets, the city's downtown Methodist congregation formed in 1838, the Greek Revival building dates from 1839 but has had a series of additions altering its original appearance.

ELSEWHERE IN FLOYD COUNTY:

MOUNT SAINT FRANCIS FRIARY, U.S. 150, near Floyds Knobs, Lafayette Township, was established in 1896 by a Catholic men's religious order, Order of Friars Minor

Second Baptist Church, New Albany, Floyd County

Saint Mary's Catholic Church, New Albany, Floyd County

Conventual, commonly known as the Conventual Franciscans. Formerly housing a seminary, the friary is the headquarters of the order's Our Lady of Consolation Province; a retreat center for laity is also here. The red brick Romanesque Revival style chapel dates from 1925. ST

★ GEORGETOWN CHURCH OF THE NAZARENE, Main Street (SR 64) and Kepley Road, Georgetown, Lafayette Township, a red brick Gothic Revival church built for United Brethren congregation in 1894.

★ ST. MARY OF THE KNOBS CATHOLIC CHURCH, 5755 St. Mary's Road, Floyd Knobs, Lafayette Township. Located in the "knobs" (hills), the congregation dates from 1823 and is the oldest parish within the Archdiocese of Indianapolis. The current red brick church was built in the Arts and Crafts style in 1908.

HARRISON COUNTY

Harrison County, located in the middle of the row of Ohio River counties, attracted early settlement and was home to the early United Brethren congregations, now part of United Methodist Church. The county attracts visitors to the Harrison-Crawford State Forest, the Wyandotte Woods and Wyandotte Caves State Recreation Areas, and the Corydon Battle Site (HABS). Today's major religious groups are Catholic, United Methodist, and Southern Baptist.

Corydon, Harrison Township, the county seat and site of the Old State Capitol building, served as Indiana's territorial capital from 1813 to 1816 then as state capital from 1816 to 1825 and has several historic churches in its vicinity:

PFRIMMER'S CHAPEL UNITED METHODIST CHURCH, 500 S. Pfrimmer's Chapel Road, south of SR 62, east of Corydon, Franklin Township, was founded by John George Pfrimmer in 1812 as Indiana's first congregation of the United Brethren in Christ. First log church was built in 1818, present church dates from 1866 but its appearance has been altered by later remodelings. Pfrimmer, who founded at least fifteen other United Brethren congregations in Indiana, and his wife, Elizabeth, are buried in the cemetery nearby. Pfrimmer's Chapel was designated a United Methodist Historic Site in 1991. ST

★ CORYDON PRESBYTERIAN CHURCH, E. Walnut and Elm streets, Corydon, Harrison Township, Gothic Revival structure built in 1906, oldest congregation in former state capital, was organized in 1819.

ELSEWHERE IN HARRISON COUNTY:

★ THOMPSON CHAPEL UNITED METHODIST CHURCH, Rothrock Mill Road near Loudens Road, Spencer Township, Greek Revival building dating from 1870, claims to be the oldest Methodist congregation with continuous service in the state, dates from 1816.

★ ST. JOHN LUTHERAN CHURCH, St. John's Church Road, Franklin Township, small building of log construction dates from 1848.

★ ST. PETER EVANGELICAL LUTHERAN CHURCH, St. Peter Church Road at Woody Lane, Franklin Township, excellent red brick Gothic Revival church built in 1880, congregation founded in 1852.

★ MOST PRECIOUS BLOOD CATHOLIC CHURCH, Fourth Street, New Middleton, Webster Township, a Mission Style church built in 1928, the parish was formed in 1880.

★ Former RIVERSIDE UNITED BRETHREN CHURCH, SR 111, 1 mile south of SR 211, Posey Township, a Greek Revival-Italianate style structure built in 1872.

ST. MARY CATHOLIC CHURCH, St. Mary's Drive and Pennington Street, Lanesville, Franklin Township, a red brick Gothic Revival church built in 1859, located on crest overlooking the town; the congregation dates from 1843.

HISTORICAL MARKER, MT. SOLOMON LUTHERAN CHURCH, SR 62 and S. Gethsemane Road, two and a half miles west of Corydon, Harrison Township, notes the founding of Indiana's first Lutheran church at a site four miles southwest in 1810, though Lutheran clergyman Rev. George Forster preached in the county as early as 1805. Mt. Solomon Church was disbanded in 1928. On the north side of SR 62 opposite marker is Gethsemane Lutheran Church, a small Gothic Revival church of native stone built in 1911.

HISTORICAL MARKER, OLD GOSHEN CHURCH SITE, SR 11 and West Old Goshen Road, north of Laconia, Boone Township, marks the site of a Baptist church built of logs around 1813 under leadership of Daniel Boone's brother, Squire Boone. The church was razed in 1963. Members of the Boone family are buried in the cemetery there, where a large memorial stone gives a history of the church and the Boones.

JACKSON COUNTY

In Jackson County the leading religious bodies are the Lutheran Church–Missouri Synod, Christian Church or Church of Christ, Church of the Nazarene, and United Methodist. Seymour, Redding Township, is the county's major center of population, though not the county seat, and the location of several of these historic churches:

★ FIRST PRESBYTERIAN CHURCH, W. 3rd and Walnut streets, is an excellent red brick Gothic Revival edifice built in 1884 for a congregation organized in 1855. NRHP

★ FIRST UNITED METHODIST CHURCH, E. 3rd and Ewing streets, is a red brick Gothic Revival church built in 1884, remodeled in 1925; the congregation was organized in 1852.

★ ST. PAUL UNITED CHURCH OF CHRIST, W. Tipton and Walnut streets, a Gothic Revival structure built in 1888 for a German Evangelical congregation formed in 1859.

★ SEYMOUR CENTRAL CHRISTIAN CHURCH, N. Chestnut and 5th streets, a church built in Neo-Classical style in 1916, the congregation organized in 1863.

★ ST. AMBROSE CATHOLIC CHURCH, S. Chestnut and South streets, a red brick Gothic Revival structure built in 1860, the year of the parish's founding.

OTHER HISTORIC CONGREGATIONS IN JACKSON COUNTY:

★ CORTLAND CHRISTIAN CHURCH, SR 258 and CR 400E, Cortland, Hamilton Township, dates from 1826 when small Methodist, Christian, and Baptist congregations shared the same building known as Cortland Union Church, the present frame Gothic Revival building dates from 1857 with extensive remodeling in 1899; now known as Cortland Christian Church.

★ HOUSTON UNITED METHODIST CHURCH, Buffalo Pike east of CR 775W, Houston, Salt Creek Township, a fine red brick Gothic Revival structure built in 1918, congregation formed in 1824.

★ ST. PAUL EVANGELICAL LUTHERAN CHURCH, 1165 E CR 400S, Wegan, Brownstown Township, a brick Romanesque Revival church dates from 1898, congregation formed in 1856.

★ FIRST PRESBYTERIAN CHURCH, E. Howard Street near Armstrong Street (U.S. 31), Crothersville, Vernon Township, a quaint wood Gothic Revival structure built in 1885, the year of the congregation's founding.

★ TRINITY LUTHERAN CHURCH, SR 135 and CR 450S, Driftwood Township, fine red brick Gothic Revival church dates from 1926, though congregation established in 1874.

★ VALLONIA UNITED METHODIST CHURCH, Main Street at CR 310W and 210S, Vallonia, Driftwood Township, red brick Gothic Revival structure built in 1906 for congregation organized in 1844.

★ MEDORA CHRISTIAN CHURCH, George and Riley streets, Medora, Carr Township, red brick Gothic Revival building dates from 1909, year of congregation's founding.

LAWRENCE COUNTY

Lawrence County and Monroe County to the north rest on a bed of world famous Indiana limestone used in construction of public and religious buildings across the country. One of the largest, the National Cathedral in Washington, D.C., is constructed with this local stone. Beautiful Spring Mill State Park attracts visitors to the county, whose major religious groups today are American Baptist, Christian Church or Church of Christ, and United Methodist.

The county seat, Bedford, Shawswick Township, is home to the following historic churches, all of limestone construction:

★ FIRST PRESBYTERIAN CHURCH, 15th and L streets, a limestone fortress with pointed and rounded arched windows suggesting Romanesque and Gothic influences. Congregation was founded in 1819, the older part of the present church was built in 1868 with extensive remodeling in 1901.

★ FIRST UNITED METHODIST CHURCH, 14th and K streets, a limestone citadel built in Gothic Revival style in 1899, congregation was organized in 1826.

★ FIRST CHRISTIAN CHURCH, 15th and K streets, south of First United Methodist, is likewise a limestone monument in Gothic Revival style, built in 1900 for congregation founded in 1846.

★ ST. VINCENT DE PAUL CATHOLIC CHURCH, Eighteenth and I streets, a limestone Gothic Revival building dating from 1893, parish founded in 1865.

OTHER SITES IN LAWRENCE COUNTY:

★ MITCHELL UNITED METHODIST CHURCH, North 8th and W. Walnut streets, Mitchell, Marion Township, congregation founded in 1856, building constructed in 1874 when it was named for Jacob Finger, the major donor. This red brick Romanesque Revival building is in magnificent condition.

★ FIRST BAPTIST CHURCH, S. 7th and W. Franklin streets, Mitchell, Marion Township, the present red brick Gothic Revival building dates from 1902; congregation organized in 1864.

★ ERIE UNITED METHODIST CHURCH, CR 150N, Erie, Shawswick Township, twentieth-century Gothic Revival church built in 1924, congregation organized in 1845.

★ JOHN GUTHRIE MEMORIAL UNITED METHODIST CHURCH, west of Tunnelton Road, Tunnelton, Guthrie Township, brick Romanesque Revival structure built in 1891, congregation dates from 1860.

ROBERTS' MEMORIAL PARK or "Rivervale," Buddha Road, North of Lawrenceport, Bono Township, the campground of the South Indiana Conference of the United Methodist Church, located on White River, established in 1924 and renamed in 1929 in honor of Bishop Robert Roberts, first Methodist bishop to reside in Indiana, whose farm was nearby. The camp buildings date from the 1920s and 1930s.

MONROE COUNTY

Monroe County, along with neighboring Lawrence County to the south, is world famous for limestone, which is used extensively in local construction including churches. The county is also famed as home of Indiana University at Bloomington and attracts visitors for recreation opportunities at Lake Monroe. The county's leading religious bodies today are Catholic, United Methodist, and Christian Church or Church of Christ.

The county seat, Bloomington, is the location of several historic religious buildings:

🏛 TIBETAN CULTURAL CENTER, 3655 Snoddy Road near Moores Creek Road on the city's southside, is situated on beautiful acreage along with the Jangchub Chorten, the only Tibetan chorten (shrine) in the United States. The Dalai Lama of Tibet dedicated the chorten in 1988. The founding figure behind Indiana's principal Buddhist site is Thubten J. Norbu, emeritus professor at Indiana University, and brother of the Dalai Lama.

🏛 ★ ANDREW WYLIE HOUSE, 2nd and Lincoln streets, is a Federal style house built in 1835. Wylie, president of Indiana University, 1829-1851, was a religious influence in the community as a Presbyterian minister who, before his death in 1851, joined the Episcopal church and was ordained. Later, his nephew, Theophilus Wylie, Indiana University professor, lived in the home and served as pastor (1838–1869) of a Reformed Presbyterian congregation in Bloomington. NRHP/HABS

★ SECOND BAPTIST CHURCH, W. 8th and N. Rogers streets, the city's first black Baptist congregation founded in 1872, the present limestone Romanesque Revival building dates from 1913. NRHP

FIRST PRESBYTERIAN CHURCH, N. Lincoln and E. 6th streets, limestone Gothic Revival building dating from 1900, congregation organized in 1819.

FIRST CHRISTIAN CHURCH, Kirkwood and E. Washington streets, an excellent limestone Gothic Revival building dates from 1917, congregation organized in 1826.

TRINITY EPISCOPAL CHURCH, W. Kirkwood and S. Grant Streets, a fine limestone church in English Gothic style built in 1909, congregation organized in 1894 with earlier antecedents.

FIRST UNITED METHODIST CHURCH, E. 4th and Washington streets, congregation founded in 1818, present monumental limestone Gothic Revival church erected in 1909.

OTHER SITES IN MONROE COUNTY:

★ FIRST UNITED METHODIST CHURCH, Temperance Street (SR 46) near Walnut Street, Ellettsville, Richland Township, limestone Romanesque Revival church dates from 1900, congregation founded in 1850.

★ FIRST BAPTIST CHURCH, Association and Sale streets, Ellettsville, Richland Township, limestone Romanesque Revival church dating from 1909.

★ MAPLE GROVE CHRISTIAN CHURCH, 5925 N. Maple Grove Road, Bloomington Township, Greek Revival building dating from 1876 with historic cemetery.

★ BETHEL CHURCH, 2609 Bethel Lane, Bloomington Township, is a fine example of carpenter built vernacular style architecture, dating from 1875 with historic cemetery.

★ CLEAR CREEK CHRISTIAN CHURCH, Rogers Street and Church Lane, Clear Creek, Perry Township, a red brick late Gothic Revival building dating from 1917 for congregation organized in 1847. Large cemetery surrounds church.

★ MT. EBAL CHURCH, 8699 Fairfax Road, Clear Creek Township, is a splendidly restored Greek Revival church built in 1872 for Methodist congregation organized in 1871, now owned and operated by a commercial enterprise that rents out the church and its facilities for social functions.

★ CHURCH OF CHRIST, First Street, Harrodsburg, Clear Creek Township, simple carpenter built structure from the late nineteenth century, congregation dates from the 1830s.

ORANGE COUNTY

Orange County's scenic hills and historic resort communities at French Lick and West Baden have drawn visitors for over a century. The latter's famous West Baden Springs Hotel (NHL/NRHP/HABSI) with its mammoth unsupported dome was site of a theological seminary of the Catholic religious order, Society of Jesus (Jesuits), from 1934 to 1964. Historic Landmarks Foundation of Indiana has undertaken the hotel's restoration. Today's leading religious bodies are Christian Church or Church of Christ, American Baptist, and United Methodist. The county seat, Paoli, is noted for its graceful Greek Revival courthouse (NRHP/HABS) and is home to these churches:

CENTRAL BAPTIST CHURCH, W. Main near N. First Street, Paoli, Paoli Township, located west of the courthouse square, is a fine red brick Gothic Revival structure.

FIRST PRESBYTERIAN CHURCH, N. E. First Street, east of courthouse square, congregation organized in 1825, the present brick Arts and Crafts style church was built in 1921.

ELSEWHERE IN ORANGE COUNTY:

AMES CHAPEL UNITED METHODIST CHURCH, U.S. 150, three miles east of West Baden, French Lick Township, lovely red brick Gothic Revival church built in 1913, congregation formed in 1879 from merger of older congregations. Historic cemetery surrounds church.

NEWBERRY FRIENDS MEETING, U.S. 150, west of Paoli, Paoli Township, excellent white frame Greek Revival building dates from 1856, historic congregation founded in 1826. NRHP

ORLEANS UNITED METHODIST CHURCH, Washington and Second streets, Orleans, Orleans Township, red brick Gothic Revival Church built in 1914, founded about 1816.

ORLEANS CHRISTIAN CHURCH, Jackson and Maple (SR 37) streets, Orleans, Orleans Township, red brick twentieth-century Gothic Revival building dating from 1920, congregation formed in 1867.

STAMPERS CREEK PRIMITIVE BAPTIST CHURCH, SR 56 east of Paoli, congregation formed in 1818, simple gable-front carpenter-built structure in excellent condition, cemetery nearby.

UNITED METHODIST CHURCH, Maple and Poplar streets, French Lick, French Lick Township, congregation founded in 1852, present imposing structure built in 1914 of brick in twentieth-century Gothic Revival style.

OUR LADY OF THE SPRINGS CATHOLIC CHURCH, Wells and Indiana streets, French Lick, French Lick Township, white frame Gothic Revival building dates from 1887, the year of parish's founding.

FIRST BAPTIST CHURCH, Elm and Sinclair streets, West Baden, French Lick Township, built in 1920 for African-American congregation whose members had service jobs in nearby resort hotels. NRHP

PERRY COUNTY

Perry County, located along the Ohio River, is noted for its rolling terrain and forms part of the Hoosier National Forest. Its major religious groups are Catholic, United Church of Christ, and American Baptist. Cannelton, Troy Township, the county seat, located on the Ohio, is home to the imposing and abandoned Cannelton Cotton Mills (NHL), a factory built in 1851. These historic churches can be found nearby:

★ ST. LUKE'S EPISCOPAL CHURCH, Washington and 3rd streets, across the street from Cannelton Cotton Mills, a white frame Greek Revival structure built in 1845 for a Unitarian congregation, later acquired by an Episcopal congregation formed in 1857. NRHP

★ FIRST UNITED METHODIST CHURCH, Taylor and 3rd streets, congregation organized in 1838, red brick Romanesque Revival church was built in 1927.

★ ST. MICHAEL CATHOLIC CHURCH, Washington and 8th streets, is an imposing sandstone Gothic Revival church dating from 1859, year of parish founding, and overlooks the town and the river.

★ ST. JOHN UNITED CHURCH OF CHRIST, Taylor and 7th streets, German Evangelical congregation was formed in 1854, the present red brick Gothic Revival church erected in 1890.

ELSEWHERE IN PERRY COUNTY:

★ HOLY CROSS CATHOLIC CHURCH, U.S. 62 at SR 37, St Croix, Oil Township, a solid Romanesque Revival building of local sandstone constructed in 1881, congregation organized in 1860.

★ ST. MARK CATHOLIC CHURCH, SR 145 about 2 miles NE of SR 37, Anderson Township, small sandstone Gothic Revival church built in 1868, parish formed in 1863.

★ EVANGELICAL UNITED CHURCH OF CHRIST, Jefferson and 10th streets, Tell City, Troy Township, red brick Romanesque Revival church built in 1906, German Evangelical immigrants formed congregation in 1866.

★ ST. PIUS CATHOLIC CHURCH, SR 66, Troy, Troy Township, red brick Romanesque Revival church built in 1883 for German Catholic congregation formed in 1847.

CHRIST OVER THE OHIO STATUE, Camp Koch on Fulton Hill, Troy, Troy Township, is a representation of Christ standing eighteen feet high with arms outstretched and overlooks Troy and the Ohio River below. The statue is the work of German sculptor Herbert Jogerst, a World War II prisoner of war at Camp Breckenridge, Kentucky, who pursued his art in Indiana after the war. The figure is cast in Terrazatine and was dedicated in 1957.

SCOTT COUNTY

One of Indiana's smaller counties, Scott County is location of Pigeon Roost State Historical Site. It has historically been the home of religious groups common in the early nineteenth century. Today's major groups include American Baptist, Christian Church or Church of Christ, and United Methodist. The county is home to these historic churches:

CHURCH OF THE NAZARENE, S. Second and E. Wardell streets, Scottsburg, Vienna Township, the county seat, is an excellent gable-front red brick building formerly a Christian Church.

OLD OX PRIMITIVE BAPTIST CHURCH, CR 400 at Big Ox Fork Creek, Finley Township, was formed in 1823, when the present gable-front church was built, reflecting simplicity of pioneer days.

LEOTA BAPTIST CHURCH, CR 300S, Leota, Finley Township, simple, frame structure with historic cemetery, congregation organized by members of Old Ox Church in 1835.

LEXINGTON PRESBYTERIAN CHURCH, Mulberry Street near Mason (SR 203), Lexington, Lexington Township, congregation organized in 1818, present church is simple Greek Revival building constructed in 1844 and remodeled in 1902.

WASHINGTON COUNTY

The Washington County seat, Salem, Washington Township, is noted as hometown of nineteenth-century U.S. Secretary of State John Hay and location of the Hay-Morrison House (NRHP/HABS). Some of the county's historic Protestant bodies were established early and remain influential. Today's major religious groups are American Baptist, Christian Church or Church of Christ, and United Methodist. Salem is home to the these fine church buildings:

FIRST BAPTIST CHURCH, Walnut and N. High streets, a fine red brick Romanesque Revival structure built in 1900, historic congregation dates from 1810. NRHP

FIRST PRESBYTERIAN CHURCH, High Street between Market and Walnut streets, red brick gable-front church built between 1839 and 1842, congregation was formed in 1817.

ELSEWHERE IN WASHINGTON COUNTY:

BLUE RIVER FRIENDS MEETINGHOUSE, SR 56 1.8 miles east of SR 135, near Salem, Washington Township, was established in 1815 when the present simple gable-front structure was built. Historical marker describes Quakers' arrival from North Carolina, bringing freed slaves with them.

HISTORICAL MARKER AND BURIAL PLACE OF JOHN WILLIAMS, SR 56, 1.2 miles east of SR 135 junction, then turn a half mile north, near Salem, commemorates an ex-slave brought from North Carolina with Quakers settling in the area. Vigilantes killed Williams at his farm here in 1863. The marker also notes the site of the African Methodist Episcopal Church once here.

LIVONIA PRESBYTERIAN CHURCH, SR 56, Livonia, Gibson Township, Greek Revival building, congregation formed in 1816, one of earliest Presbyterian congregations organized in the state.

Southeast Region

DEARBORN COUNTY

Dearborn County, with two substantial communities on the Ohio River—Lawrenceburg and Aurora—began settlement in the early nineteenth century. The county's historic religious profile is reflected in today's leading groups: Catholic, American Baptist, and United Methodist. Lawrenceburg, the county seat, is home to the magnificent Classical style courthouse (NRHP/HABSI) and these historic church buildings:

🏛 ★ HAMLINE UNITED METHODIST CHURCH, High and Vine streets, historic congregation formed in 1806, the present Greek Revival building of exceptional beauty was built in 1847. The church is named for noted nineteenth-century Methodist writer, editor, and bishop, Leonidas Hamline. NRHP

★ BEECHER PRESBYTERIAN CHURCH, Short Street, red brick building in Queen Anne style dates from 1882, congregation founded in 1829, and renamed in 1929 for Henry Ward Beecher, one of the most famous American Protestant clergymen of the nineteenth century. His first ministerial appointment was here from 1837 to 1839 before moving to Second Presbyterian Church in Indianapolis.

★ HARRY LELAND ZERBE LAW BUILDING, 15 W. Center Street, only a few blocks from Hamline Church, is a fine Greek Revival structure built in 1860 for German Methodist congregation formed in 1839.

★ ZION UNITED CHURCH OF CHRIST, Walnut between Center and Tate streets, founded as German Evangelical Church, present buff brick Greek Revival building dates from 1867.

★ ST. LAWRENCE CATHOLIC CHURCH, Walnut Street and Eads Parkway, congregation founded in 1842, present buff brick building in Romanesque Revival style dates from 1868.

Aurora, Center Township, is the location of majestic Hillforest (NHL/HABS/NRHP), the historic house of industrialist Thomas Gaff, built 1852–1856, now a museum overlooking the city. Aurora is also home to these beautiful historic churches:

★ FIRST UNITED METHODIST CHURCH, 3rd near Main Street, a splendid Greek Revival building dating from 1857–1863, congregation formed in 1816.

★ FIRST PRESBYTERIAN CHURCH, 4th and Main streets, a stately painted brick Greek Revival structure dating from 1847, congregation formed in 1844. NRHP

★ ST. MARY CATHOLIC CHURCH, 4th and Judiciary streets, adjacent to First Presbyterian Church, congregation formed in 1857, present red brick Gothic Revival church built in 1864.

★ FIRST EVANGELICAL UNITED CHURCH OF CHRIST, 5th and Market streets, founded as a German Evangelical congregation, present red brick Gothic Revival building dates from 1874. NRHP

ST. JOHN EVANGELICAL LUTHERAN CHURCH, Mechanic Street between 2nd and 3rd streets, a red brick Gothic Revival structure built in 1874, congregation formed in 1860.

★ JESSE L. HOLMAN-MARY O'BRIEN GIBSON HOUSE, "Veraestau," SR 56 one mile south of Aurora, Jesse Holman was a Baptist leader and a founder of Franklin College. NRHP/HABS

OTHER HISTORIC PLACES IN DEARBORN COUNTY:

★ ROUTE 46 PENTECOSTAL CHURCH, SR 46, 1 mile west of SR 1, Kelso Township, a native stone Gothic Revival structure built in 1867 for St. Paul Evangelical Lutheran Church.

★ ST. JOHN THE BAPTIST CATHOLIC CHURCH, 25740 SR 1, Dover, Kelso Township, red brick Romanesque Revival church completed in 1879 for a congregation founded in 1824.

★ ST. PAUL CATHOLIC CHURCH, 9795 N. Dearborn Road, New Alsace, Kelso Township, parish dates from 1833, present brick Romanesque Revival church dates from 1837 with later additions.

★ ST. JOSEPH CATHOLIC CHURCH, SR 1 and Church Lane, St. Leon, Kelso Township, congregation dates from 1841, the present red brick Gothic Revival church was built in the early 1860s.

★ ST. MARTIN CATHOLIC CHURCH, 8075 Yorkridge Rd., near Guilford, York Township, congregation dates from 1850, present red brick Romanesque Revival church built in 1915.

★ PENTECOSTAL WORSHIP CENTER, A Street, Guilford, York Township, founded as Methodist congregation, the carpenter built structure dates from 1899.

★ EAST FORK BAPTIST CHAPEL, East Fork Road off SR 1, near Guilford, Miller Township, was built in Federal style in 1821 and is reputed to be Indiana's oldest house of worship still in use. The congregation was founded about 1811 and belonged to Methodist Protestant conference 1829–1938.

★ CARNEGIE HALL, 14687 W. Main Street, Moores Hill, Sparta Township, was built in 1907 with funding from Andrew Carnegie. It formerly housed Moores Hill College that was founded by Methodist Conference in 1854. The college was moved to Evansville in 1917 to become Evansville College. NRHP.

UNITED METHODIST CHURCH, W. Main and Manchester streets, Moores Hill, Sparta Township, congregation founded 1818, the fine Greek Revival building dates from 1870–1871.

ST. JOHN LUTHERAN CHURCH, N. Dearborn Road near Lawrenceville Road, Hubbells Corner, Jackson Township, red brick Gothic Revival church was built in 1905. Historical marker describes St. John's as possibly the second oldest worshipping Lutheran congregation in Indiana. Known also as Hubbell's Church, congregation was formed in 1833 and is mother church of the area's Missouri Synod Lutheran churches.

DECATUR COUNTY

Decatur County is home to historic religious bodies which have been present since the nineteenth century. In the county's present religious profile, the leading groups are Catholic, American Baptist, and United Methodist. Greensburg, Washington Township, the county seat, is famed for the tree growing in the courthouse tower (NRHP/HABSI) and home to these fine churches:

FIRST PRESBYTERIAN CHURCH, N. Franklin and E. Washington streets, on courthouse square, dedicated in 1881, built in red brick Gothic Revival style, its soaring bell tower rivals the courthouse tower. Congregation formed in 1826.

FIRST UNITED METHODIST CHURCH, Broadway and North streets, congregation established in 1823, the splendid limestone Neo-Gothic church was built in 1926.

FIRST CHRISTIAN CHURCH, N. Broadway and Hendricks streets, Gothic Revival building with perma stone exterior dates from 1868, congregation dates from 1832.

ST. MARY CATHOLIC CHURCH, East and McKee streets, a fine red brick Gothic Revival church dating from 1884, congregation was formed in 1858.

OTHER SITES IN DECATUR COUNTY:

WESTPORT CHRISTIAN CHURCH, W. Mulberry and Range streets, Westport, Sand Creek Township, red brick Romanesque Revival edifice built in 1912, congregation organized in 1850.

WESTPORT BAPTIST CHURCH, E. Main and N. West streets, Westport, Sand Creek Township, magnificent red brick twentieth-century Classical Revival building dates from 1915, congregation organized in 1851.

FIRST UNITED METHODIST CHURCH, N. East at E. Mulberry streets, Westport, Sand

Creek Township, built in 1892 and rebuilt in 1916 in Classical Revival style, congregation dates from 1851.

SAND CREEK BAPTIST CHURCH, U.S. 421 and CR 300S, Marion Township, red brick gable-front building dating from 1883 with additions in 1923 and several thereafter, oldest Baptist church in the county dates from 1822.

MT. PLEASANT UNITED METHODIST CHURCH, CR SW60, 4 miles south of Greensburg, Marion Township, this carpenter built church dating from 1858 is the oldest in continuous use in the county, congregation formed in 1834.

UNION BAPTIST CHURCH, CR 400S near SW60, Marion Township, white carpenter built structure dates from late nineteenth century, congregation formed in 1825.

ST. PAUL EVANGELICAL LUTHERAN CHURCH, CR 550E near 400S, Smyrna, Salt Creek Township, excellent red brick Gothic Revival structure dating from 1866 with additions, congregation formed in 1861.

NEW POINT CHRISTIAN CHURCH, CR 200S, New Point, Salt Creek Township, red brick gable-front building dating from 1870, congregation was organized in 1862.

ST. MAURICE CATHOLIC CHURCH, near CR 850E and 150N, St. Maurice, Fugit Township, founded in 1857, Romanesque Revival church built in 1882.

ST. JOHN THE EVANGELIST CATHOLIC CHURCH, 2204 County Line Road, Enochsburg, Salt Creek Township, on the Decatur-Franklin County line. This congregation began in 1844, its Gothic Revival building in native stone dates from 1858.

IMMACULATE CONCEPTION CATHOLIC CHURCH, 2081 East CR 820S, Millhousen, Marion Township, red brick Romanesque Revival building dates from 1866–1868, congregation was organized in 1834.

FRANKLIN COUNTY

Franklin County in the Whitewater River valley attracted settlers from the early nineteenth century and flourished in the 1830s and 1840s during the heyday of the Whitewater Canal. German immigrants to the area gave the county a strong German Catholic character. Today the county attracts visitors to Brookville Lake State Reservoir and the Whitewater Canal Historic Site (HABS) at Metamora. The leading religious bodies are Catholic, United Methodist, and independent congregations.

🏛 ★ LITTLE CEDAR GROVE BAPTIST CHURCH, U.S. 52, two miles south of Brookville, Brookville Township, oldest church building at its original location in the state, simple red brick structure built in 1812. Building includes rifle holes in the exterior walls. The Franklin County Historical Society renovated and owns building, no longer home of an active congregation. NRHP/HABS

Little Cedar Grove Baptist Church, Cedar Grove, Franklin County

Brookville, the county seat, is located on a bluff over the Whitewater River, and is the site of a choice group of church buildings:

★ OLD BROOKVILLE CHURCH or OLD BRICK CHURCH AND CEMETERY, 10th and Franklin streets, first permanent church in Brookville, built in 1820 for Methodists who worshipped there until 1839. Then successive congregations used it for worship: Presbyterians 1839–1855, Lutherans 1855–1922, Baptists since 1953. Building now is property of the Franklin County Historical Society. Many early Brookville settlers are buried in the surrounding cemetery including four Revolutionary War soldiers and one signer of Indiana's first constitution.

ST. MICHAEL CATHOLIC CHURCH, High and 3rd streets. Red brick Gothic Revival structure dates from 1862, enlarged in 1902. Congregation formed in 1845. Historical Marker describes the site as former home of U.S. Senator James Noble and Indiana Governor Noah Noble. A marker at the adjacent property on the north notes the home of David Wallace, an Indiana governor and father of General Lew Wallace, author of *Ben-Hur*.

BROOKVILLE UNITED METHODIST CHURCH, Church and 8th streets, a splendid red brick Gothic Revival building dates from 1883, congregation formed in 1833.

ST. THOMAS LUTHERAN CHURCH, Franklin and 9th streets, red brick Gothic Revival church built in 1929, congregation was organized in 1848.

CHURCH OF CHRIST, Franklin and 10th streets, brick twentieth-century Gothic Revival church built in 1917, congregation established in 1886.

🏛 OLDENBURG, the "Village of Spires," Ray Township, is noted for its distinctive German and Catholic character as reflected in domestic architecture and religious sites:

★ CHAPEL OF THE IMMACULATE CONCEPTION, Main and Pearl streets, an imposing red brick Victorian Baroque structure built in 1889 according to design of D. A. Bohlen, serves as place of worship for Franciscan Sisters.

★ CONVENT OF THE IMMACULATE CONCEPTION, adjoining the above, is an imposing red brick Victorian Romanesque structure built in 1901 according to design of Bohlen firm of Indianapolis. The Sisters of St. Francis, a Catholic religious order, established a convent here in 1851 under leadership of Rev. Francis Joseph Rudolf, Oldenburg's pastor, and Mother Theresa Hackelmeier, an immigrant from Vienna, Austria. The sisters' primary work has been the staffing of Catholic schools at first in the local area and later in several states.

★ HOLY FAMILY CATHOLIC CHURCH, Main and Pearl streets, opposite Immaculate Conception Chapel described above, red brick Victorian Gothic building dates from 1861, parish founded in 1837.

★ "OLD STONE CHURCH," the earlier HOLY FAMILY CHURCH, Pearl Street, behind

Old Brookville Church and Cemetery, Brookville, Franklin County

the "new" parish church described above, a Romanesque Revival structure of native stone built between 1846–1848, then was part of friary building until 1985 when it was renovated as present parish rectory.

HISTORICAL MARKER, Pearl and Water streets, notes site of OLDENBURG FRIARY, demolished in 1985, which at various times housed the novitiate and theological seminary of the St. John the Baptist (Cincinnati) Province of the Catholic men's religious order, the Order of Friars Minor (Franciscans).

★ MATER DOLOROSA SHRINE, Shrine Road, east of Oldenburg, Ray Township, small Victorian Gothic chapel built in 1871 by Siegfried Koehler, a pious German Catholic immigrant.

ELSEWHERE IN FRANKLIN COUNTY:

★ ST. NICHOLAS LUTHERAN CHURCH, SR 229 and Beacon Road, Peppertown, Salt Creek Township, red brick Gothic Revival church built in 1875, the year of congregation's founding.

★ Former CUPP CHURCH AND CEMETERY, Cupp Road near SR 229, Metamora Township, Greek Revival structure built in 1850, longtime home of Methodist congregation.

★ MEETINGHOUSE ANTIQUES, along the Canal in Metamora, Metamora Township, founded as Metamora Christian Church where Christian Restoration movement leader Alexander Campbell visited and preached. Congregation built Greek Revival building in 1871.

★ FRANKLIN UNITED METHODIST CHURCH, Franklin Road near SR 101, Fairfield Township, Greek Revival structure built in 1871, founded as United Brethren congregation in 1824. NRHP

★ GUARDIAN ANGEL CATHOLIC CHURCH, U.S. 52, Cedar Grove, Highland Township, an imposing red brick Gothic Revival edifice dates from 1896, parish established in 1872.

★ ST. CECILIA OF ROME CATHOLIC CHURCH, St. Mary's Road, Oak Forest, Butler Township, formerly called St. Philomena Church, Gothic Revival structure built in 1870, congregation formed in 1844.

★ ST. MARY OF THE ROCK CATHOLIC CHURCH, 17440 St. Mary's Road, Butler Township, brick Gothic Revival structure was built in 1890, congregation formed in 1844.

ST. JOHN'S UNITED CHURCH OF CHRIST (Huntersville Church), Columbus Avenue and Huntersville Road, Ray Township, Batesville, (most of which is in Ripley County), red brick Romanesque Revival edifice with lovely spire built in 1859 with additions in 1888, congregation founded as Evangelical Lutheran Church in 1836.

JEFFERSON COUNTY

Jefferson County on the Ohio River is the location of Clifty Falls State Park, whose rugged beauty draws visitors. The county's early settlement brought to the area the religious denominations prominent in nineteenth-century America. Today's major religious bodies include American Baptist, Catholic, and United Methodist.

Madison, the picturesque county seat, was one of the state's leading cities before the Civil War owing to the economic advantages of its Ohio River location. With 133 blocks in the Madison Historic District (HABS), the city is a treasure trove of Indiana's best examples of early architecture especially the state's finest Classical Revival mansion, the James F. D. Lanier State Historic Site (NRHP/NHL). Included among the fine buildings are the following excellent churches:

🏛 ★ MADISON PRESBYTERIAN CHURCH, Broadway and First streets, Classical style church was built in 1848 for First Presbyterian congregation formed in 1815. In 1833, Second Presbyterian was formed from it; congregations reunited in 1921. HABS

🏛 ★ HISTORIC MADISON INC., E. Third and West streets. This spectacular temple was built for the former Second Presbyterian congregation in 1834, the first major Greek Revival building in Madison, designed by Edwin J. Peck. HABS

🏛 ★ FIRST BAPTIST CHURCH, Vine Street between Main and Third streets, considered the city's oldest congregation, was formed in 1807 and is also reputed to be the oldest Baptist church in continuous existence in Indiana. Located at present site since 1830, its splendid Classical Revival building was constructed between 1853 and 1860. HABS

🏛 ★ CHRIST EPISCOPAL CHURCH, Mulberry Street between Third and Fourth streets, brick Gothic Revival building constructed in 1848–1850, designed by Cincinnati architect W. Russell West, parish formed in 1834. HABS

🏛 ★ Former ST. MICHAEL CATHOLIC CHURCH, E. Third and St. Michael's streets, congregation dates from 1837, the Gothic Revival church of native stone was completed in 1839 according to design of noted Madison architect Francis Costigan. Building may be the oldest Gothic Revival style house of worship in the state. St. Michael parish was merged with nearby St. Mary's parish to form Prince of Peace Catholic parish in 1993. Next to church is the rectory (HABS) also designed by Costigan and built ca. 1860. Church and rectory are property of Historic Madison, Inc.

★ TRINITY UNITED METHODIST CHURCH, Broadway between Main and Third streets, red brick Gothic Revival structure was built 1872–1874, congregation dates from 1873.

★ PRINCE OF PEACE CATHOLIC CHURCH, E. Second between Walnut and East streets, formerly St. Mary Catholic Church, a German Catholic congregation organized in 1850, the church is a painted-brick Gothic Revival building completed in 1851;

Saint Michael Church (former), Madison, Jefferson County

merged with two other Catholic parishes in 1993 to form congregation under new name.

★ Former St. PATRICK CATHOLIC CHURCH, State Street near Michigan Road, founded on Madison's north side in 1853, the present red brick Gothic Revival church dates from 1910. It was merged to form Prince of Peace Catholic parish in 1993.

EBENEZER UNITED METHODIST CHURCH, 409 Poplar, is historically a black congregation of the United Methodist Church, construction date not certain. Greek Revival building renovated as a church with Gothic windows, congregation dates from 1834.

St. JOHN UNITED CHURCH OF CHRIST, 501 E. Main Street, formerly the church for the German Methodist congregation. Dating from 1842, the present simple Classical revival-style building was constructed 1848–1850.

SECOND BAPTIST CHURCH (site of), Broadway Street near Presbyterian Avenue, red brick Gothic Revival structure built in 1883 for city's black Baptists. Demolished in June 1996.

FIRST CHRISTIAN CHURCH, W. Main and Vine streets, red brick Gothic Revival building whose nineteenth-century appearance has been altered by additions and renovations.

SHERMAN, BARBER, AND MULLIKIN CERTIFIED PUBLIC ACCOUNTANTS, W. Third between Poplar and Broadway streets, fine Greek Revival building founded as Roberts Methodist Episcopal Chapel in 1844.

Hanover, Hanover Township, on SR 56–62, west of Madison, is a picturesque old town noted for well preserved historic buildings and its historic Presbyterian sites. ST

🏛 ★ JOHN FINLEY CROWE HOUSE, Crowe Street near Presbyterian Avenue, is the well preserved twelve-room frame home of the Presbyterian clergyman and Hanover College founder, built in 1829. (NRHP/HABS) Historical Marker, in front of this private residence, designates the site of the log cabin where John Finley Crowe opened Hanover Academy in 1827.

HANOVER PRESBYTERIAN CHURCH, Main Street near Presbyterian Avenue, is a stately gable-front Gothic Revival/Italianate building, its earlier parts date from 1832 with later additions, located in the heart of Hanover.

🏛 HANOVER COLLEGE, a coeducational liberal arts institution, is Indiana Presbyterians' historic institution of higher learning and the oldest private college in the state. Founded as Hanover Academy in 1829 by John Finley Crowe, pastor of Hanover's Presbyterian church, the school was rechartered as Hanover College in 1833. The college was relocated from the heart of Hanover to its present site in 1883. Most campus buildings were built after 1940, but the colonial style of archi-

Hanover Presbyterian Church, Hanover, Jefferson County

tecture leaves the impression that the campus is older. Its location on a bluff overlooking the Ohio River and its wooded landscape make it one of the state's most attractive campuses.

HANOVER COLLEGE YMCA BUILDING, on the above campus, west side of Lucina Ball Drive, north of Prospect Street. This gable-front wood structure built in 1883 was the first YMCA established on a college campus in the United States. HABS

ELSEWHERE IN JEFFERSON COUNTY:

★ ELEUTHERIAN COLLEGE, SR 250, Lancaster, Lancaster Township, a large three-story stone building in Classical style that housed the second school west of the Allegheny Mountains after Oberlin College in Ohio to offer interracial education. Founded in 1848, the college had close ties to the local Neal Creek Abolition Baptist Church. The present building was completed in 1856, and the college closed in 1874. Its most notable alumnus was Rev. Moses Broyles, pastor of Second Baptist Church in Indianapolis and a founder of the Indiana Association of Black Baptist Churches.

★ DUPONT UNITED METHODIST CHURCH, W. Main Street near SR 7, Dupont, Lancaster Township, Gothic Revival church built in 1908, congregation dates from 1830.

LIBERTY CHRISTIAN CHURCH, U.S. 421 near Thornton Road, Belleview, Monroe Township, gable-front building dates from 1842 with additions in 1910 and 1941. It is said to be the state's oldest Christian Church (that is, the Christian denomination), organized in 1817, originally located on the grounds of the nearby Jefferson Proving Grounds and relocated in 1940.

★ HOPEWELL CHURCH, CR 700W near 300N, Volga, Smyrna Township, stone gablefront structure built in 1848 with historic cemetery.

JENNINGS COUNTY

Jennings County's leading religious groups are American Baptist, Catholic, and United Methodist. The Jennings County seat, Vernon, is home to a splendid Italianate style courthouse, built in 1859, the centerpiece of the picturesque Vernon Historic District (HABSI) that is coextensive with the town. Vernon once enjoyed regional influence through these churches:

★ VERNON BAPTIST CHURCH, Washington and Perry streets, Italianate style church built in 1871, congregation dates from 1815 when the Baptist minister John Vawter founded Vernon.

VERNON PRESBYTERIAN CHURCH, Washington Street near Montgomery, congregation established in 1825, the graceful Greek Revival structure was built in 1832.

★ VERNON SEMINARY (Presbyterian), near Presbyterian church is a Greek Revival building dating from 1850, but a private residence since 1860.

North Vernon, Center Township, is the county's largest municipality where these historic churches are located:

★ FIRST BAPTIST CHURCH, S. State and Chestnut streets, is a magnificent twentieth-century Gothic Revival church built in 1905, congregation was founded in 1835.

★ ST. MARY CATHOLIC CHURCH, Clay and Washington streets, red brick Gothic Revival church dates from 1861, the year of parish's founding.

★ NORTH VERNON PRESBYTERIAN CHURCH, Jennings and Chestnut streets, is a small Gothic Revival building dating from 1871, congregation organized in 1870.

OTHER SITES IN JENNINGS COUNTY:

★ ST. ANNE CATHOLIC CHURCH, CR 150E, Sand Creek Township, red brick Gothic Revival church built in 1866, parish formed in 1841.

★ ST. JOSEPH CATHOLIC CHURCH, CR 700W and 200S, Buena Vista, Spencer Township, red brick Gothic Revival structure built in 1892, parish formed in 1850.

OHIO COUNTY

Located on the Ohio River, the state's smallest county and its county seat, Rising Sun, in Randolph Township, were settled in the early nineteenth century. The county courthouse, a Greek Revival structure built in 1845, is the state's oldest in continuous use. Today's leading religious bodies are Christian Church or Church of Christ, American Baptist, and United Methodist. Rising Sun is home to these fine churches:

★ Former FIRST PRESBYTERIAN CHURCH, Main Street near Walnut Street, Romanesque Revival church dates from 1832, congregation organized in 1816.

★ FIRST UNITED CHURCH OF CHRIST, N. High and Fifth streets, red brick Italianate building constructed in 1880, congregation dates from 1869.

★ UNITED METHODIST CHURCH, Walnut Street between Second and Main streets, congregation founded in 1821, red brick Greek Revival church dates from 1865.

RIPLEY COUNTY

Ripley County with an economy based on agriculture and industry also attracts visitors to Versailles State Park. Today's leading religious bodies are Catholic, Evangelical Lutheran Church of America, and American Baptist. Batesville, Laughery Township, though not the county seat, is the county's largest population center and location of these fine church buildings:

★ ST. MARK EVANGELICAL LUTHERAN CHURCH, W. Pearl and Vine streets, formed in 1897, when members of Huntersville Church west of Batesville seceded. Present red brick Gothic Revival church constructed in 1897–1898.

★ BATESVILLE BAPTIST CHURCH, E. Catherine and Sycamore streets, formerly Bethany English Evangelical Lutheran Church, Jacobean Revival style building dates from 1913.

★ UNITED METHODIST CHURCH, Park Avenue and South Street, was founded as a German Methodist congregation in 1870, the splendidly preserved red brick Gothic Revival building dates from 1889.

★ ST. LOUIS CATHOLIC CHURCH, St. Louis Place and Walnut Street, an imposing red brick Gothic Revival church, dating from 1868, the year of parish's founding. Its soaring spire dominates Batesville skyline.

OTHER SITES IN RIPLEY COUNTY:

🏛 ★TYSON UNITED METHODIST CHURCH, W. Tyson and S. Adams streets, Versailles, Johnson Township, is a splendid example of the Art Deco style and was built in 1936–1937 of aluminum with no nails. James Tyson, Versailles native and a co-founder of the Walgreen drugstore chain, had this fine church built as a memorial to his mother, Elizabeth Adams Tyson. The county seat's historic Methodist congregation dates from 1834.

★ ST. JOHN'S UNITED CHURCH OF CHRIST, SR 101 and CR 1300 N, Penntown, Adams Township, founded as German Evangelical church in 1840, present red brick Gothic Revival building dates from 1901.

★ ST. NICHOLAS CATHOLIC CHURCH, 6461 E. St. Nicholas Drive, near Sunman, Adams Township, is a red brick Gothic Revival church dating from 1856, congregation formed in 1836.

★ ST. ANTHONY CATHOLIC CHURCH, E. Church Street near SR 46, Morris, Adams Township, stately red brick Romanesque Revival church dates from 1885, parish was organized in 1855.

★ ST. MAURICE CATHOLIC CHURCH, Harrison Street, Napoleon, Jackson Township, Gothic Revival Church built in 1869 for congregation founded in 1848.

★ OSGOOD UNITED METHODIST CHURCH, 232 Walnut Street, Osgood, Center Township, congregation organized in 1856, present church dates from 1878 but was rebuilt in Colonial Revival style in 1931.

Tyson United Methodist Church, Versailles, Ripley County

★ St. John the Baptist Catholic Church, Buckeye Street, Osgood, Center Township, parish dates from 1867 with present Renaissance Revival church built in 1914.

★ St. Paul Lutheran Church, SR 129, Olean, Brown Township, red brick Romanesque Revival church built in 1921, congregation established in 1857.

Switzerland County

Switzerland County takes it name from the homeland of nineteenth-century French-speaking Swiss immigrants who settled this Ohio River county. The county's largest religious bodies today are American Baptist, United Methodist, and Catholic. Vevay, the picturesque county seat located on the Ohio River, is the home of several fine church buildings:

★ Ruter Chapel United Methodist Church, W. Main and N. Union streets, magnificent red brick Classical Revival building dates from 1859, congregation formed in 1816.

★ Switzerland County Historical Museum, E. Main and Market streets, former Presbyterian Church founded in 1828, the present red brick Gothic Revival building dates from 1860.

★ Switzerland Baptist Church, Main Cross and W. Pike streets, red brick Romanesque Revival gem facing the courthouse square dates from 1873.

★ Most Sorrowful Mother Catholic Church, N. Ferry and Jackson streets, red brick gable-front structure built in 1875, the year of parish's founding.

Elsewhere in Switzerland County:

★ East Enterprise United Methodist Church, SR 56 near SR 250, East Enterprise, Cotton Township, Federal style structure built around 1864, congregation dates from 1834.

★ Fairview United Methodist Church, Fairview Road, Fairview, Cotton Township, frame Gothic Revival church built in 1870 by congregation founded in 1816.

★ Caledonia Presbyterian Church, Caledonia Road, Pleasant Township, congregation dates from 1820, first church built 1828, present structure is in the Arts and Crafts style built in 1920.

★ Bennington United Methodist Church, Main Street, Bennington, Pleasant Township, carpenter built Gothic Revival church dates from 1870, congregation was started in 1838.

★ Former Mt. Zion Methodist Episcopal Church, Little Doe Run west of

Braytown Road, Craig Township, is a Vernacular Primitive structure built in 1878.

★ FREDONIA REGULAR BAPTIST CHURCH, Tapps Ridge Road, Jefferson Township, a simple gable-front building of native stone built in 1855.

Southwest Region

Daviess County

The county's leading religious bodies are Catholic, Christian Church or Church of Christ, and United Methodist. Washington, the county seat, is home to some of the county's most distinguished religious buildings:

★ St. Simon Catholic Church, E. Hefron and NE Third streets, the present ornate red brick Gothic Revival church dates from 1886, parish formed in 1837.

★ First Baptist Church, E. Walnut Street and NE First streets, Neo-Classical building dates from 1914 for congregation started in 1840.

★ First Christian Church, E. Walnut and NE Third streets, Romanesque Revival building dates from 1896 and rebuilt after fire of 1912, congregation formed in 1864.

★ St. Mary Catholic Church, W. Van Trees and NW Second streets, founded for Washington's German-speaking Catholics in 1873, when the present red brick Gothic Revival church was built.

★ Central Christian Church, W. Van Trees and NW First streets, is a Tudor Revival building dating from 1928–1929, when congregation was formed.

★ Washington Catholic High School, NE Second and Walnut streets, red brick Mission style edifice built around 1925.

Other Sites in Daviess County:

★ Former Pleasant Hill United Brethren Church, CR 1550N and 900E, north of Odon, Madison Township, Gothic Revival style church built in 1891 for United Brethren congregation, surrounded by historic cemetery.

★ Elnora United Methodist Church, Meridian and Main streets, Elnora, Madison Township, an excellent yellow brick Romanesque Revival church built in 1910, congregation founded in 1875.

★ St. Peter Catholic Church, Second Street near Church Street, Montgomery, Barr Township, founded in 1818, one of the state's oldest Catholic parishes. Here, French émigré priest, Edward Sorin, and his Brothers of Holy Cross spent their first year (1841–1842) in the United States, before relocating to St. Joseph County to open the University of Notre Dame. Red brick Gothic Revival church here, built in 1865, is located on a crest overlooking the town.

★ ST. PATRICK CATHOLIC CHURCH, CR 800E near 500S, Corning, Reeve Township, founded in 1840 for Irish immigrants in area, present red brick Gothic Revival church dates from 1860.

DUBOIS COUNTY

Dubois County's early settlers were Scotch-Irish with waves of German immigrants soon following to give the area its distinctive character. Today's leading religious groups reflect its German heritage with a population that is heavily Catholic. The other leading religious bodies are the Evangelical Lutheran Church of America and the United Church of Christ. The county is home to an exceptional number of fine religious buildings:

🏛 MONASTERY IMMACULATE CONCEPTION, 802 E. 10th Street, Ferdinand, Ferdinand Township, convent of Catholic women's religious order, Sisters of St. Benedict, and their college preparatory high school for girls, Marian Heights Academy. The founding German-speaking sisters came to Ferdinand in 1867 from Covington, Kentucky to staff St. Ferdinand parish school and other parish schools in the vicinity. The imposing complex of red brick buildings that includes convent, academy, and church crown a hill, Mount Tabor, and is visible for miles. The red brick Romanesque Revival church designed by St. Louis architect Victor Klutho was completed in 1924. NRHP

🏛 SHILOH CAMP GROUND or OLD ALEXANDER'S CAMP MEETING SITE, southeast of Ireland on Shiloh Road near CR 150N, Madison Township. The county's early Scotch-Irish settlers started this former Cumberland Presbyterian congregation in 1817. The well maintained gable-front church building dates from 1849 and the cemetery from 1860. Together they form a picturesque site in a wooded setting. NRHP

🏛 ST. JOSEPH CATHOLIC CHURCH, Newton Street between 11th and 13th streets, Jasper, Bainbridge Township, is a massive sandstone Romanesque Revival building seating a thousand, one of the largest churches in southern Indiana, built from 1867 to 1880. German Catholic settlers formed the parish in 1837; its early pastor, Joseph Kundek, recruited German Catholic immigrants to settle in Jasper and founded surrounding communities and churches for them. NRHP

Huntingburg, Patoka Township, is the county's second largest city after the county seat, Jasper, and location of several historic congregations:

SALEM UNITED CHURCH OF CHRIST, 4th and Walnut streets, originated as a German Evangelical congregation in 1842. The imposing and graceful red brick Gothic Revival structure was built in 1870.

ST. MARY CATHOLIC CHURCH, Washington Street at E. Franklin Street, is a well maintained red brick Gothic Revival building dating from 1884, congregation formed in 1862.

FIRST BAPTIST CHURCH, Geiger and 4th streets, red brick Gothic Revival building constructed for congregation of Emmanuel Evangelical Church in 1867, a congregation formed in 1841.

HUNTINGBURG UNITED METHODIST CHURCH, Main and 5th streets, red brick Classical Revival building constructed in 1922 for congregation formed in 1850.

OTHER SIGNIFICANT SITES IN DUBOIS COUNTY:

LEMMON'S PRESBYTERIAN CHURCH, W. Portersville Road near CR 750W, near Portersville, Boone Township, founded by Cumberland Presbyterians in 1859, building constructed and dedicated in 1860. Historic cemetery surrounds the church. NRHP

Former EMMANUEL LUTHERAN CHURCH, CR 445E and 600N, 1 mile south of SR 56, near Dubois, Harbison Township, known locally as Hill Church, congregation was formed in 1858, gable-front Gothic church built in 1901. Community organization now owns church building. NRHP

ST. FERDINAND CATHOLIC CHURCH, 840 Maryland Street, Ferdinand, Ferdinand Township, is located down the hill from Monastery Immaculate Conception, cited above. Congregation founded among German Catholics in 1840. Sandstone Romanesque Revival church dating from 1845 boasts fine oil portraits of Swiss artist Paul Deschwanden inside. Town and church honor patron saint of Austrian Emperor Ferdinand I.

ST. PAUL UNITED CHURCH OF CHRIST, CR 800S east of SR 161, near Holland, Cass Township, founded as German Evangelical congregation in 1840, red brick Gothic Revival church dates from 1869 with later additions.

ST. HENRY CATHOLIC CHURCH, CR 1100S, St. Henry, Cass Township, red brick Romanesque Revival structure dates from 1910, congregation formed in 1862.

ST. ANTHONY CATHOLIC CHURCH, 4444 Ohio Street, St. Anthony, Jackson Township, parish and its sandstone Romanesque Revival building date from 1864.

ST. MARY CATHOLIC CHURCH, CR 500W, Ireland, Madison Township, red brick Gothic Revival building dates from 1904, parish formed in 1891.

SACRED HEART CATHOLIC CHURCH, 2504 Walnut Street, Schnellville, Jefferson Township, parish dates from 1873, present brick Gothic Revival church built in 1916.

ST. JAMES LUTHERAN CHURCH, Iowa and 2nd streets, Holland, Cass Township, red brick Gothic Revival building dates from 1875, congregation formed in 1852.

GIBSON COUNTY

The leading religious bodies in Gibson County include the General Baptist, whose modest houses of worship dot the county, as well as Catholic and United Methodist. The following religious sites and buildings can be found in the county:

OAKLAND CITY COLLEGE, W. Washington Street, Oakland City, Columbia Township, the centerpiece of the General Baptist movement in Indiana is this coeducational liberal arts college. Chartered in 1885, the college's Administration Building dates from 1892. The attractive College Chapel of modern design faces Elm Street.

AT PRINCETON, PATOKA TOWNSHIP, THE COUNTY SEAT:

GRAVE OF NICHOLAS SNETHEN, Warnock Cemetery, N. Main and E. Warnock streets, is an Official United Methodist Historic Site. Snethen (1769–1845) entered the ministry of the Methodist Episcopal Church in 1794. In 1800 he was chosen to travel with Bishop Francis Asbury and became known as "Francis Asbury's Silver Trumpet." Later Snethen actively opposed the episcopal form of church polity and supported lay representation in all councils of the church. He presided over the organizing conference of the Associated Methodist Churches that became the Methodist Protestant Church in 1830. His grave marker resembles a pulpit with carved stone "Bible" open on top.

★ FIRST PRESBYTERIAN CHURCH, W. Water and S. Hart streets, an excellent red brick Romanesque Revival structure built in 1894, congregation formed in 1828.

★ BROADWAY CHRISTIAN CHURCH, E. Broadway and S. Prince streets, founded 1889, twentieth-century Romanesque Revival church built in 1925.

★ FIRST UNITED METHODIST CHURCH, N. West and W. Emerson streets, excellent red brick Romanesque Revival edifice built in 1894, congregation was started in 1815.

UNITED PRESBYTERIAN CHURCH, E. State and N. Prince streets, organized in 1810 as Reformed Presbyterian congregation, the present red brick Romanesque Revival church was built in 1858 and rebuilt in 1897.

ELSEWHERE IN GIBSON COUNTY:

★ ST. JAMES CATHOLIC CHURCH, CR 1275S and 25W, Old Princeton Road, Johnson Township, congregation founded in 1847, the imposing red brick Romanesque Revival church building dates from 1855, its tower visible for miles to motorists on U.S. 41 and I-64.

WAYMAN CHAPEL AFRICAN METHODIST EPISCOPAL CHURCH, CR 100N and 500W, Lyles Station, Patoka Township, is a simple carpenter built church dating from 1887 and remodeled in 1952. Lyles Station, founded before the Civil War by free African

Americans, was once a thriving community, now nearly deserted. Wayman Chapel is one of few rural AME churches left in the state.

KNOX COUNTY

The Knox County seat, Vincennes, is the state's oldest permanent European settlement. Its founding around 1732 marks the beginning of St. Francis Xavier parish for French Catholic settlers, the first Christian congregation in the state. Once the capital of the Indiana Territory, Vincennes is home to the Territorial Capitol of Former Indiana Territory (HABSI) and Old State Bank (NRHP/HABSI) state historic sites as well as the George Rogers Clark National Historical Park (NRHP). Today the county's religious profile reflects its religious heritage with leading groups, Catholics, United Methodists, and American Baptists.

The Vincennes Historic District (HABS) and its vicinity are the locations of these historic churches and sites:

🏛 ST. FRANCIS XAVIER CATHOLIC BASILICA, 2nd and Church streets, a graceful red brick Classical Revival building. As the congregation's third church, it was started in 1826 and largely finished by 1841. It served as cathedral church for the diocese of Vincennes from 1834 to 1898 when the title of the Catholic diocese was transferred to Indianapolis. Also in the complex of buildings is the former library, the present Bruté Library housing rare book collections of the first Catholic bishop of Vincennes, Simon Bruté de Rémur, as well as St. Rose Chapel and rectory. NRHP/HABS/ST

🏛 GROUSELAND, Parker and Scott streets, the home of Indiana Territorial Governor William Henry Harrison, later President of the United States, was built in 1802–1804, and was home for Harrison and his family until 1812. Harrison invited visiting Protestant clergy to conduct services in the council chamber at Grouseland in view of the lack of Protestant houses of worship in Vincennes. NRHP/HABS/NHL/ST

MARIA CREEK BAPTIST CHURCH, Harrison near 2nd Street, Vincennes University campus, commemorates the state's second Baptist congregation founded in 1809 at a site north of city. This replica of that congregation's early brick house of worship was built in 1970 and serves as the University's interdenominational chapel. ST

FIRST UNITED METHODIST CHURCH, N. 4th and Perry streets, present imposing limestone Romanesque Revival structure built in 1899, rebuilt in 1918 for congregation formed in 1809, one of oldest Methodist congregations in the state.

FIRST BAPTIST CHURCH, N. 5th and Broadway streets, is an imposing twentieth-century Classical Revival building constructed for the city's historic Baptist church, congregation organized in 1862.

FIRST PRESBYTERIAN CHURCH, N. 5th and Busseron streets, founded in 1833, daughter congregation of the state's oldest Presbyterian church, Indiana Presbyterian

Saint Francis Xavier Catholic Basilica, Vincennes, Knox County

Church, southeast of Vincennes (see below). The present Gothic Revival building was constructed in 1898. Historical Marker on church exterior notes that the Indiana Synod of the Presbyterian Church was formed at Vincennes in 1826.

ST. JOHN THE BAPTIST CATHOLIC CHURCH, Main Street near N. 8th Street, founded for the city's German Catholics, is a red brick Gothic Revival building dating from 1851 with spire completed later.

ST. JAMES EPISCOPAL CHURCH, N. 6th and Perry streets, a graceful English Gothic limestone building constructed in 1907, parish organized in 1839.

ST. JOHN EVANGELICAL LUTHERAN CHURCH, S. 8th and Scott streets, red brick Gothic Revival structure built in 1870, formed for German immigrants in 1848 as Evangelical and Lutheran congregation.

ST. JOHN UNITED CHURCH OF CHRIST, N. 5th and Shelby streets, formed in 1859 when German Evangelical members withdrew from the congregation above. The red brick Gothic Revival structure was constructed in 1886–1887.

BETHANY PRESBYTERIAN CHURCH, S. 8th and Shelby streets (opposite St. John Evangelical Lutheran Church), is a red brick Gothic Revival church constructed in 1907, congregation organized in 1890.

NEAR VINCENNES:

🏛 INDIANA PRESBYTERIAN CHURCH, SR 61 and CR SE150, Palmyra Township, was organized following a visit by Rev. Thomas Cleland in 1805; he preached in the council chamber at Grouseland at the invitation of William Henry Harrison. The Presbyterian congregation thereafter formed in 1806 met for worship at a farm near Vincennes before present brick Gothic Revival building was begun in 1844. Indiana Presbyterian is reputed to be the oldest Protestant congregation in the area of the Northwest Territory in continuous service. Tower added in 1909. American Presbyterian/Reformed Historical Site.

UPPER INDIANA PRESBYTERIAN CHURCH, 4500 Old Bruceville Road, Palmyra Township, organized as part of the preceding congregation in 1806 which met at several worship sites. Present church built in 1913 on scenic eleven-acre site.

ST. THOMAS CATHOLIC CHURCH, near U.S. 41 at CR 1000S and CR 500W, frame Gothic Revival building in excellent condition, dates from 1843–1844, tower added in 1913.

ST. VINCENT DE PAUL CATHOLIC CHURCH, Hart Street, Highland, founded in 1849 as clerical seminary for the diocese of Vincennes, then served as diocesan orphanage from 1860 to 1972. The present Romanesque Revival parish church was built in 1927.

Maria Creek Baptist Church, Vincennes, Knox County

Indiana Presbyterian Church, Palmyra Township, Knox County

ELSEWHERE IN KNOX COUNTY:

HISTORICAL MARKER, SHAKER PRAIRIE, SR 41 and CR 1100N, near Oaktown, Busseron Township, commemorates the Shaker community that developed near here between 1811 and 1812, and from 1814 to 1827.

FIRST CHRISTIAN CHURCH, Third and School streets, Oaktown, Busseron Township, is a well preserved red brick Romanesque Revival church dating from 1905–1906, congregation organized in 1866.

CHRISTIAN CHURCH, SR 550, on the west side of Bruceville, Washington Township, is a red brick Romanesque Revival building, congregation started in 1841.

BAPTIST CHURCH, Washington and 4th streets, Bicknell, Vigo Township, was founded in 1870 and its home is a twentieth-century Classical Revival building.

FIRST CHRISTIAN CHURCH, Freelandville Avenue and Third Street, Bicknell, Vigo Township, founded in 1874, housed in a fine Classical Revival building.

FIRST CHRISTIAN CHURCH, Anderson and McGinnis streets, Sandborn, Vigo Township, is a splendid Classical Revival building dating from the early twentieth century, congregation founded in 1880s.

SALEM UNITED CHURCH OF CHRIST, 1st Street, north of Junction of SR 67 and SR 58, Westphalia, Vigo Township, founded as a German Evangelical congregation in 1850. Red brick Gothic Revival building dates from 1920.

FIRST BAPTIST CHURCH, 5th Street near Jefferson Street, Edwardsport, Vigo Township, congregation formed in 1858, red brick Gothic Revival church built in 1890.

PRESBYTERIAN CHURCH, Main and Eleventh streets, Monroe City, Harrison Township, superb red brick Romanesque Revival edifice built in 1895, organized as Cumberland Presbyterian congregation in 1858.

BETHEL UNITED CHURCH OF CHRIST, SR 58 near CR 1100N, east of Freelandville, Widner Township, founded as German Evangelical congregation in 1900, the present fine red brick Gothic Revival building dates from 1934.

MARTIN COUNTY

Much of Martin County's scenic landscape is under federal control within the Crane Naval Weapons Support Center or the Hoosier National Forest. The Martin State Forest is the county's major attraction to visitors. The county's leading religious bodies are Catholic, United Methodist, and Christian Church or Church of Christ. These are some of the county's noteworthy religious buildings:

ST. MARTIN CATHOLIC CHURCH, U.S. 231, Whitfield, Center Township, frame carpenter built church dates from 1875, congregation founded in 1845.

LOOGOOTEE UNITED METHODIST CHURCH, Main Street, Loogootee, Perry Township, Gothic Revival building dates from 1906, congregation organized in 1858.

ST. JOHN CATHOLIC CHURCH, Church Street, Loogootee, Perry Township, red brick Gothic Revival church built in 1880, parish founded in 1860.

SHOALS CHRISTIAN CHURCH, 6th and Main streets, Shoals, Halbert Township, Gothic Revival structure built in 1911, congregation dates from 1860.

SHOALS UNITED METHODIST CHURCH, 5th & Main streets, Shoals, Halbert Township, Romanesque Revival church built in 1900, the year of congregation's founding.

ST. JOSEPH CATHOLIC CHURCH, near U.S. 231, Bramble, Brown Township, present frame Gothic Revival church built in 1875, congregation dates from 1854.

PIKE COUNTY

Pike County is noted for coal mining and electric power plants and home to the Pike State Forest. Leading church bodies are General Baptist, United Methodist, Catholic, and American Baptist. The following historic churches deserve attention:

MAIN STREET PRESBYTERIAN CHURCH, 10th and Main streets, Petersburg, Washington Township, founded as a Cumberland Presbyterian congregation in 1821 in the Pike county seat, present red brick Gothic Revival building dates from 1886.

SS. PETER AND PAUL CATHOLIC CHURCH, 8th and Sycamore streets, Petersburg, Washington Township, red brick Romanesque Revival church built in 1924, parish dates from 1847.

WINSLOW CHRISTIAN CHURCH, Walnut and Lafayette streets, Winslow, Patoka Township, organized 1893, red brick twentieth-century Romanesque Revival church built in 1923.

WINSLOW UNITED METHODIST CHURCH, Cherry and Lafayette streets, Winslow, Patoka Township, red brick Romanesque Revival building dates from 1928, congregation formed in 1854.

SPURGEON GENERAL BAPTIST CHURCH, near SR 61, Spurgeon, Monroe Township, organized in 1859, gable-front red brick structure rebuilt 1953.

SPURGEON UNITED METHODIST CHURCH, SR 61, Spurgeon, Monroe Township, twentieth-century Gothic Revival building dates from 1924, congregation established in 1856.

POSEY COUNTY

Posey County, located in the southwestern extremity of Indiana, is famed as location of New Harmony, one of the nineteenth century's famous experiments in communal living, and Harmonie State Park. Leading religious bodies are Catholic, United Methodist, and United Church of Christ. The county boasts a selection of historic and unique buildings:

🏛 NEW HARMONY HISTORIC DISTRICT, SR 66, Harmony Township, is the site of historic buildings related to two experiments in communal living. The first one, Harmonie, embodied the vision of George Rapp and his followers. Rapp, who had dissented from the teachings and practices of the Lutheran state church in his native Württemberg, led his followers to the United States in 1805. They settled in Butler County, Pennsylvania where they set up a model community to share religious and economic life. In 1814, Rapp and his followers relocated their colony along the banks of the Wabash in Posey County. By 1824, the site proved unsuitable for the Harmonists and they sold it and returned to Pennsylvania. The buyer was Robert Owen, a Welsh textile manufacturer and philanthropist. He renamed the town New Harmony and established a community to live by his socialist vision. His experiment lasted from 1825–1827. NHL/HABS

ATHENEUM/VISITORS' CENTER, North Street, New Harmony, provides orientation film, information on tours, and a map of sites for a walking tour of this splendidly preserved town.

★ ROOFLESS CHURCH, W. North and Main streets, imaginative interdenominational church of modern design commemorating New Harmony's religious heritage. World-class architect Philip Johnson designed the structure in park-like brick enclosure, completed in 1960. Artist Jacques Lipchitz designed the very striking decorative gates and the Madonna sculpture in the church.

TILLICH PARK, near E. North and N. Main streets, is the location of the grave of the great twentieth-century Protestant theologian, Paul Tillich (1886–1965). Selections from his writings are carved in stone tablets on the grounds.

★ HOLY ANGELS CATHOLIC CHURCH, S. Main and W. South streets, frame Gothic Revival church built in 1899, the year of the parish's founding.

★ Former GERMAN SALEM CHURCH, N. First and E. Granary streets, well preserved white carpenter built Gothic Revival building constructed around 1870.

JOHNSON UNITED METHODIST CHURCH, N. Raintree and E. Granary streets, red brick Gothic Revival structure built in 1905, congregation founded in 1845.

Roofless Church, New Harmony, Posey County

ST. STEPHEN EPISCOPAL CHURCH, N. Main and Granary streets, limestone Gothic Revival church built in 1911, congregation founded in 1841.

Mt. Vernon, Black Township, the county seat located on the Ohio River, is the location of these fine churches:

★ FIRST PRESBYTERIAN CHURCH, 6th Street between Main and Walnut streets, red brick Gothic Revival church built in 1872, congregation formed in 1839.

★ TRINITY CHURCH OF CHRIST, E. 5th Street between Main and Walnut streets, fine red brick Gothic Revival building dates from 1884, congregation formed as German Evangelical in 1853.

★ ST. MATTHEW CATHOLIC CHURCH, Walnut and 5th streets, red brick Romanesque Revival structure built in 1879, congregation established in 1857.

POSEY COUNTY'S OTHER SITES:

★ UNITED CHURCH OF CHRIST, North and Walnut streets, Cynthiana, Smith Township, red brick Romanesque revival church built by local resident L. J. Wilkinson in 1901, year of congregation's founding.

★ ZION LIPPE UNITED CHURCH OF CHRIST, Copperline Road and CR 900E, Robinson Township, fine red brick Gothic Revival edifice built in 1895, founded as German Evangelical congregation in 1843.

ST. PAUL UNITED METHODIST CHURCH, St. Phillip Road near Sunset Drive, Marrs Township, this fine gable-front rural church dates from 1911 for congregation formed in 1844.

★ ST. PHILLIP CATHOLIC CHURCH, St. Phillip Road, St. Phillip's, Marrs Township, red brick Romanesque Revival edifice built in 1859, parish dates from 1847.

★ ST. JOHN UNITED METHODIST CHURCH, Caborn (CR 700E) and Middle Evansville-Mt. Vernon Road (CR 415S), Marrs Township, an excellent frame Gothic Revival gem, built in 1887, established as German Methodist congregation in 1843.

★ Former SALEM CHURCH, Welborn Road, Marrs Township, frame Gothic Revival built in 1888 for German Evangelical congregation. Current Salem United Church of Christ located on Lower Mt. Vernon Road, 2 miles south of SR 62.

ST. WENDEL CATHOLIC CHURCH, St. Wendel and Boonville-New Harmony roads, Robinson Township, fine red brick Romanesque Revival church built in 1854, parish dates from 1842.

POSEYVILLE CHRISTIAN CHURCH, Main (SR 135) and Oak streets, Poseyville, Robb Township, fine brick twentieth-century Classical Revival building.

ST. PAUL'S UNITED METHODIST CHURCH, Cole and Oak streets, Poseyville, Robb Township, red brick Gothic Revival structure built in 1904, congregation organized in 1816.

ST. FRANCIS XAVIER CATHOLIC CHURCH, N. St. Francis Avenue and Main Street (SR 135), Poseyville, Robb Township, red brick Romanesque Revival edifice, congregation formed in 1886.

SPENCER COUNTY

Spencer County is famed as Abraham Lincoln's boyhood home—suitably commemorated at Lincoln Boyhood Home National Memorial (NHL/NRHP) and Lincoln State Park. Jones House State Historic Site at Gentryville recalls Lincoln's employment at William Jones' store. The county also became the home to large numbers of German immigrants settling in the nineteenth century. Major religious groups today include Catholic, Christian Church or Church of Christ, and United Methodist. The county also boasts some of the following excellent religious sites:

ST. MEINRAD ARCHABBEY AND SEMINARY, near SR 62 and SR 545, St. Meinrad, Harrison Township, is a monastery of the Order of St. Benedict (Benedictines), a Catholic men's monastic order. The monastic community conducts a seminary consisting of a liberal arts college and school of theology preparing candidates for ministry in the Catholic Church. The seminary attracts a national student body. Monks from Einsiedeln Abbey in Switzerland established the monastery in 1854 and opened seminary in 1861. Church of Our Lady of Einsiedeln was built in Romanesque Revival style in 1899–1907. The major buildings are constructed with native sandstone and reflect European and modern styles. The present monastery and library of contemporary design by Evans Woollen date from the 1980s. ST

OUR LADY OF MONTE CASSINO CHAPEL, SR 62 and Monte Cassino Road, east of St. Meinrad, Harrison Township, is a small sandstone Romanesque Revival chapel built in 1868–1870 as a local place of pilgrimage by monks and students of nearby St. Meinrad Archabbey and Seminary.

ELSEWHERE IN SPENCER COUNTY:

TRINITY UNITED METHODIST CHURCH, 5th and Walnut streets, Rockport, Ohio Township, is an exceptionally graceful red brick Gothic Revival building, constructed for the county seat's historic Methodist congregation dating from 1822.

ST. BERNARD CATHOLIC CHURCH, Elm and N. 6th streets, Rockport, Ohio Township, is a red brick Gothic Revival Church in excellent condition begun in 1875, congregation dates from 1850.

Former GERMAN EVANGELICAL ST. PAUL'S CHURCH, SR 245 at CR 1600N south of Santa Claus, Huff Township, is a small well maintained carpenter built church build-

Saint Meinrad Archabbey, Saint Meinrad, Spencer County

ing dating from 1880. No longer serving an active congregation, the building commemorates the German settlement in the area. NRHP

SANTA CLAUS UNITED METHODIST CHURCH, near SR 245 at CR 600N and 1675E, Carter Township, northwest of Santa Claus, founded as Salem German Methodist Episcopal Church in 1849. Gothic Revival church was built in 1873. This historic German congregation is located at campgrounds founded in 1851 that originally served the German Methodist Conference.

ST. BONIFACE CATHOLIC CHURCH, SR 545, Fulda, Harrison Township, fine Gothic Revival church built in 1866 for congregation of German Catholics founded in 1847. NRHP

KRATZBURG-TRINITY UNITED CHURCH OF CHRIST, SR 545 and CR 1475N, near Fulda, Harrison Township, a gable-front frame white church with historic cemetery, founded as German Evangelical congregation.

MARY HELP OF CHRISTIANS CATHOLIC CHURCH, near SR 62, Mariah Hill, Carter Township, is a Romanesque Revival building of native sandstone constructed in 1864–1865, parish formed in 1860.

ST. JOSEPH CATHOLIC CHURCH, Maple and Wallace streets, Dale, Carter Township, is a red brick Romanesque Revival building that overlooks the town and dates from 1909, the year of parish's founding.

ST. JOHN CHRYSOSTOM CATHOLIC CHURCH, near SR 545, New Boston, Huff Township, frame Romanesque Revival church built in 1862 for congregation formed in 1859.

ST. MARTIN CATHOLIC CHURCH, Church and Spring streets, Chrisney, Grass Township, small red brick Romanesque Revival edifice in excellent condition dates from 1898.

VANDERBURGH COUNTY

Vanderburgh County is home to southern Indiana's metropolis, Evansville, "the Crescent City," located on a bend on the Ohio River. The county's major religious bodies are Catholic, Southern Baptist, United Church of Christ, and United Methodist. The following religious sites and buildings can be found in the Evansville area:

🏛 ANGEL MOUNDS STATE HISTORIC SITE, 8215 Pollack Avenue, is a partial reconstruction of a village once home to 1,000 Middle Mississippian Indians living at the site in the 14th and 15th centuries. Among the buildings is the village's place of worship. This is the state's most important site depicting Indian religion. NRHP/NHL

Angel Mounds State Historic Site, Evansville, Vanderburgh County

🏛 UNIVERSITY OF EVANSVILLE, 1800 Lincoln Avenue between Rotherwood and Weinbach streets, Evansville, formerly Evansville College, is a coeducational United Methodist university dating from 1917 when Indiana Methodists moved Moores Hill College from Moores Hill, Dearborn County, to Evansville.

★ OLMSTEAD ADMINISTRATION HALL (NRHP), the historic building on the University of Evansville campus, is a fine limestone Collegiate Gothic building dating from 1921–1922. Among the university's other excellent buildings is Neu Chapel located on the campus's westside.

CHURCHES IN DOWNTOWN EVANSVILLE:

★ LIBERTY BAPTIST CHURCH, Oak Street and Martin Luther King, Jr. Boulevard, city's oldest black congregation in continuous existence, its first church at the site was built in 1865, the current brick Gothic Revival church was built in 1882, heavily damaged by a tornado and rebuilt in 1886. NRHP

★ ZION EVANGELICAL UNITED CHURCH OF CHRIST, 415 N.W. Fifth Street, formerly German Evangelical church, built in Gothic Revival style of red brick in 1855, interior extensively remodeled in 1893 and 1952. Rev. Heinrich Toelke, German Evangelical leader in southwestern Indiana, was pastor.

★ FIRST PRESBYTERIAN CHURCH, S.E. Second and Mulberry streets, originally Grace Presbyterian Church, is a fortress-like Gothic Revival building with two massive towers, built in 1873. The congregation, organized in 1821, is the city's oldest.

★ ST. PAUL'S EPISCOPAL CHURCH, S.E. First and Chestnut streets, was built in 1885 in an appealing English Gothic style of Bedford limestone, congregation organized in 1836. Gutted by fire in 1938, the church's walls remained and the interior was rebuilt.

★ ST. MARY CATHOLIC CHURCH, Cherry and S.E. Sixth streets, the oldest extant Catholic church in the city dates from 1867, built in Gothic Revival style with perma stone facade.

★ TRINITY UNITED METHODIST CHURCH, S.E. Third and Chestnut streets, is a fine English Gothic building dating from 1866, and patterned after the Chestnut Street Methodist Church in Newark, New Jersey; congregation dates from 1825.

★ FIRST BAPTIST CHURCH, Cherry and S.E. Fourth Streets, a fine red brick twentieth-century Classical Revival structure built in 1921, congregation organized in 1847. Congregation's earlier building stands a block away at Cherry and S.E. Third streets, built in 1867–1869; later used as B'nai Moshe congregation and by other congregations, now unused.

★ ST. JOHN UNITED CHURCH OF CHRIST, Third and Ingle streets, twentieth-century Gothic Revival structure dates from 1921 with limestone facing added in 1950 that

Olmstead Administration Hall, University of Evansville, Evansville, Vanderburgh County

alters its original appearance. The congregation was founded as German Evangelical church in 1850.

★ BETHANY APOSTOLIC CHURCH, formerly First Church of Christ, Scientist, 212 E. Mulberry Street, between Second and Third streets, a limestone Neoclassical style house of worship dating from 1915.

ELSEWHERE IN EVANSVILLE:

HOWELL GENERAL BAPTIST CHURCH, 1820 Delmar Street, is a red brick Neo-Classical structure built in 1916. The congregation, dating from the 1820s, is first one formed by Benoni Stinson, founding leader of Indiana's own General Baptist denomination.

★ HOWELL UNITED METHODIST CHURCH, 1408 Stinson Avenue, English cottage style structure dates from 1940, congregation organized in 1892.

★ TRINITY LUTHERAN CHURCH, 1000 W. Illinois between Third and Fourth streets, a stately Gothic Revival building dating from 1870, congregation organized in 1847.

★ EMMANUEL EVANGELICAL LUTHERAN CHURCH, First Avenue and Franklin Street, is a handsome red brick Gothic Revival church dating from 1856.

★ ST. ANTHONY CATHOLIC CHURCH, First Avenue and Columbia Street, a stately red brick Romanesque Revival church with two soaring towers dating from 1894, congregation formed in 1888.

★ ST. LUCAS UNITED CHURCH OF CHRIST, 33 W. Virginia Avenue, is an excellent Gothic Revival church begun in 1889, founded as German Evangelical congregation.

★ ST. PAUL LUTHERAN CHURCH, Michigan Street and Elsas Avenue, fine brick twentieth-century Gothic Revival building dates from 1907 for congregation formed in 1887.

★ ST. BONIFACE CATHOLIC CHURCH, 418 N. Wabash Avenue, parish started in 1880, a stately red brick Romanesque Revival edifice was built in 1882, gutted by fire in 1902, and rebuilt similar to original.

★ ST. BONIFACE CONVENT, nearby at 2017 W. Michigan, is a red brick Colonial Revival structure dating from 1907.

★ SACRED HEART CATHOLIC CHURCH, 2715 W. Franklin Street near Mt. Vernon Avenue, red brick Colonial Revival structure built 1928, parish formed in 1885.

★ NAZARENE MISSIONARY BAPTIST CHURCH, 867 Walnut Street at Bedford Avenue, formerly Olivett Presbyterian Church, a red brick Romanesque Revival structure dating from 1912. The congregation, founded in 1919, has worshipped here since 1968.

★ CALVARY CHAPEL, 816 Jefferson Avenue near Evans Avenue, a stately limestone Tudor Revival building dating from 1924, was formerly Redeemer Lutheran Chapel and School.

★ WASHINGTON AVENUE PRESBYTERIAN CHURCH, 641 Washington Avenue at Morton Avenue, a yellow brick twentieth-century Gothic Revival church built in 1913.

★ WORD OF LIFE CHURCH, 430 W. Washington Avenue, an imposing brick twentieth-century Gothic Revival structure dating from 1914, was formerly St. Mark's Lutheran Church.

★ MT. ZION BAPTIST CHURCH, 800 Blackford Avenue, twentieth-century Gothic Revival church built in 1908 for African American congregation dates from the 1880s.

★ EVANSVILLE CHRISTIAN LIFE CENTER AND NEW LIFE COMMUNITY CHURCH, 509 S. Kentucky Avenue, occupy a red brick Gothic Revival complex consisting of church and residence dating from 1897. The buildings are former home of Monastery of St. Clare, a convent of the Catholic women's religious order, Order of St. Clare.

★ REITZ MEMORIAL CATHOLIC HIGH SCHOOL, 1500 Lincoln Avenue, between Bennighof and Runnymeade avenues, occupies a yellow brick and limestone Collegiate Gothic style building dates from 1923 and is gift of Catholic layman Francis Reitz.

ST. BENEDICT CATHOLIC CHURCH, 1328 Lincoln Avenue, is a massive Italian Renaissance Revival building constructed in 1927–1928 and is the city's largest Catholic church, parish dates from 1912.

★ ST. BENEDICT SCHOOL, nearby at 530 S. Harlan Avenue, is a red brick Neo-Classical structure built in 1913–1914.

ADATH B'NAI ISRAEL TEMPLE, 3600 E. Washington Street, limestone building of contemporary design built in 1955, congregation formed at downtown location in 1883.

NORTHERN VANDERBURGH COUNTY:

OLD NORTH UNITED METHODIST CHURCH, 4201 Stringtown Road, Center Township, the oldest remaining church structure in Evansville, is a gable-front carpenter built structure dating from 1834, for congregation formed in 1831; the congregation worships in adjoining church building dates from 1953.

★ MCCUTCHANVILLE UNITED METHODIST CHURCH, Kansas Road and Erskine Lane, McCutchanville, Scott Township, founded as McJohnston Chapel, on grounds of congregation's present modern church, is a small, fine red brick Gothic Revival structure built in 1880, for congregation formed in 1840. NRHP

★ ST. JOSEPH CATHOLIC CHURCH, St. Joseph and St. Wendel roads, German Township, red brick Gothic Revival structure in excellent condition dates from 1888, parish was organized in 1841.

★ SALEM UNITED CHURCH OF CHRIST, 13143 Princeton Road, Darmstadt, Scott Township, Gothic Revival building dates from ca. 1880, founded as German Evangelical congregation, ca. 1860.

WARRICK COUNTY

Warrick County on the Ohio River is home to a number of historic communities. Religious groups most influential in the county today are Catholic, United Methodist, and Southern Baptist. Boonville, the Warrick County seat, is home to the following distinguished churches:

★ HEMENWAY MEMORIAL PRESBYTERIAN CHURCH, N. 4th and Sycamore streets, Boon Township, congregation organized in 1866, named for the prominent Hemenway family whose generosity sustained the church. Present Classical Revival building dates from 1919–1920.

MAIN STREET UNITED METHODIST CHURCH, N. 5th and E. Main streets, fine red brick Gothic Revival building erected in 1905 for historic congregation formed in 1829.

ST. JOHN UNITED CHURCH OF CHRIST, Sycamore and N. 6th streets, red brick Romanesque Revival church built in 1901 for German Evangelical congregation.

ST. CLEMENT CATHOLIC CHURCH, Sycamore and N. 7th streets, stucco Gothic Revival structure built in 1880–1882 when parish was established.

ELSEWHERE IN WARRICK COUNTY:

★ NEWBURGH TOWN HALL, N. State and W. Main streets, Newburgh, Ohio Township, founded as congregation of Cumberland Presbyterians, once numerous in southern Indiana; carpenter built structure dates from 1851. NRHP

★ ST. RUPERT CATHOLIC CHURCH, 1244 Red Brush Road, Newburgh, Anderson Township, red brick Romanesque Revival church dates from 1902, parish founded in 1865.

LYNNVILLE UNITED METHODIST CHURCH, 200 E. Third Street, Lynnville, Hart Township, congregation dates from 1840s, Gothic Revival church built in 1919.

BARNETT'S CHAPEL CHURCH, 6500 Meinert Road, Lynnville, Hart Township, frame white Gothic Revival church built in 1910, jointly used by Methodist and Baptist congregations founded in early nineteenth century.

ST. MATTHEW UNITED CHURCH OF CHRIST, Route 1, Lynnville, Hart Township, simple white gable-front Gothic Revival building dates from 1877, congregation formed in 1862.

West Central Region

Clay County

Clay County's diversified economy includes farming, coal mining, and industry. Its leading religious bodies are today United Methodist, Christian Church or Church of Christ, and American Baptist. The county seat, Brazil, has a set of church buildings representing some of the area's historic faiths:

FIRST UNITED METHODIST CHURCH, N. Meridian and W. State streets, organized as Hendrix Chapel in 1839, red brick Romanesque Revival building of monumental quality erected in 1900.

FIRST PRESBYTERIAN CHURCH, N. Walnut and Dr. Daniel Biggs streets, a well designed dark brick Gothic Revival church built in 1923, congregation founded in 1850.

CHURCH OF CHRIST, SCIENTIST, N. Walnut and Dr. Daniel Biggs streets, small Classical Revival building erected in 1919.

ANNUNCIATION CATHOLIC CHURCH, E. Church and N. Alabama streets, Gothic Revival perma stone structure erected in 1880, parish formed in 1860.

Clay City, Harrison Township, is the substantial community in southern Clay County with several historic congregations:

FIRST UNITED METHODIST CHURCH, 7th and Washington streets, a red brick Romanesque Revival structure in excellent condition dating from 1897, congregation formed in 1886.

EIGHTH STREET UNITED METHODIST CHURCH, Eighth and Washington streets, founded as United Brethren congregation in 1887, its red brick Gothic Revival building dates from 1923.

FIRST CHRISTIAN CHURCH, E. Columbus and S. Monroe streets, established in 1857, burned and rebuilt in 1925, orange brick church with antebellum appearance.

Also Visit:

🏛 POLAND HISTORIC CHAPEL, SR 42 near CR 56S, Poland, Cass Township. This splendidly preserved carpenter built structure dates from 1869 and evokes the simplicity of worship space in small-town and rural Protestant churches of the nineteenth century. The building was home to a Presbyterian congregation formed in 1816. Chapel is now operated by the local community and open daily. NRHP

FOUNTAIN COUNTY

Fountain County is home to one of the state's important natural wonders, Portland Arch. This rural county's religious past is reflected in today's leading religious groups, United Methodist, Christian Church or Church of Christ, and Catholic. Attica, Logan Township, the major center of population, though not the county seat, is a well preserved historic town on the Wabash River and home to these fine churches:

★ FIRST LUTHERAN CHURCH, E. Pike and S. Brady streets, is a graceful Greek Revival building dating from 1859, congregation founded by Swedish immigrants.

★ ST. FRANCIS XAVIER CATHOLIC CHURCH, S. Perry and W. Monroe streets, is a fine red brick Gothic Revival structure built in 1890, parish dates from 1862.

★ ATTICA-WILLIAMSPORT PRESBYTERIAN CHURCH, E. Main and Sixth streets, a splendid red brick Tudor Gothic Revival church built in 1906, congregation organized in 1843. In recent years it has merged with the Presbyterian congregation located in nearby Williamsport, Warren County.

★ THE OLD CHURCH, E. Main Street between Sixth and McDonald streets, next to the above church, is a beautifully restored Greek Revival gem built in 1849 for the Presbyterian church, then used as a Church of Christ, Scientist, for many years until Historic Landmarks of Fountain County restored it. Old Church now serves as a community center.

★ FIRST UNITED METHODIST CHURCH, E. Jackson and S. Brady streets, red brick Italian Renaissance Revival building with campanile, built in 1920 for congregation organized in 1828.

BETHEL CHURCH AND GRAVEYARD, Bethel Road near Riverside Road east of Attica, is a Methodist congregation established in 1825, present simple structure was built in 1830. Historic marker in cemetery relates church's history. NRHP

ELSEWHERE IN FOUNTAIN COUNTY:

★ HOPEWELL BAPTIST CHURCH, W. Clay and Adams streets, Newtown, Richland Township, red brick Romanesque Revival structure built in 1905, congregation started in 1835.

★ OSBORN PRAIRIE CHRISTIAN CHURCH (UNITED CHURCH OF CHRIST), CR 300N near 70W, near Stone Bluff, Van Buren Township, congregation founded in 1838, present red brick Gothic Revival church dates from 1891–1892, cemetery surrounds building.

★ BONEBRAKE CORNER CHURCH, CR 300S and U.S. 41, Van Buren Township, local church built in functional style in 1847 for a United Brethren congregation formed

The Old Church, Attica, Fountain County

in 1828, used for many years as a non-denominational church until 1901 and as a school. Historic cemetery is at the site.

★ FIRST CHRISTIAN CHURCH, N. Mill and W. 3rd streets, Veedersburg, Van Buren Township, is a fine red brick Classical Revival building dating from 1901, congregation formed in 1874.

★ COVINGTON UNITED METHODIST CHURCH, Washington and 5th streets, Covington, Troy Township, red brick Gothic Revival structure built in 1889, for congregation formed at the Fountain County seat in 1828.

★ FIRST CHURCH OF CHRIST, Fifth Street near Crockett Street, Covington, Troy Township, red brick Gothic Revival church built in 1901, congregation dates from 1853.

★ PRAIRIE CHAPEL CHRISTIAN CHURCH, CR 500S and 600E, a half mile east of SR 341, Cain Township, frame Gothic Revival structure built in 1904, congregation organized in 1868.

★ PHANUEL EVANGELICAL LUTHERAN CHURCH, CR 1000S, 1 mile east of SR 341, Wallace, Jackson Township, congregation was organized in 1832 among German settlers who arrived from North Carolina in 1828. The fine brick church with Gothic Revival and Neo-Classical elements dates from 1917. Situated on rolling terrain, church and historic cemetery form an especially beautiful scene.

GREENE COUNTY

Greene County's religious past is reflected today by leading church bodies: American Baptist, United Methodist, and Christian Church or Church of Christ. Linton, Stockton Township, though not the county seat, is the county's largest center of population and site of these fine church buildings:

SARON UNITED CHURCH OF CHRIST, D Street NE and 1st Street NE, founded as a Reformed congregation in 1854, dark brick Classical Revival building dates from 1916.

FIRST CHRISTIAN CHURCH, Main Street NW and C Street NW, an impressive red brick Romanesque Revival building dating from 1909.

Former CHURCH OF JESUS CHRIST OF LATTER DAY SAINTS, D Street NW and 1st Street NW, building dates from 1952, the first Latter Day Saints (Mormon) congregation in Indiana started in the early twentieth century.

FIRST UNITED METHODIST CHURCH, B Street NE and 2nd Street NE, eclectic limestone Gothic and Romanesque style building dates from 1903, congregation organized in 1823.

OTTERBEIN UNITED METHODIST CHURCH, E. Vincennes and 3rd Street NE, formerly a United Brethren congregation founded in 1901, red brick Classical Revival church built in 1922.

AT BLOOMFIELD, THE COUNTY SEAT:

FIRST METHODIST CHURCH, W. Main and Jefferson streets, red brick twentieth-century Gothic Revival structure built in 1924 for congregation established in 1845 with antecedents to 1825.

Former FIRST PRESBYTERIAN CHURCH, W. Main and Jefferson streets, across from First Methodist, not currently used as church, red brick Gothic Revival edifice built in 1896–1898 for congregation formed by Cumberland Presbyterians in 1823.

CHURCH OF THE NAZARENE, S. Franklin and Mechanic streets, formerly First Baptist Church until 1979, red brick Gothic Revival structure completed in 1923. First Baptist was organized in 1869; First Nazarene in 1915.

OTHER SITES IN GREENE COUNTY:

FOLSOM MEMORIAL UNITED METHODIST CHURCH, E. Main and S. Lafayette streets, Worthington, Jefferson Township, is an excellent brick Romanesque Revival structure built in 1900, congregation founded in 1833.

FIRST CHRISTIAN CHURCH, E. Main and S. Lafayette streets (opposite the above), Worthington, Jefferson Township, fine red brick Neo-Classical building dates from 1914–1915, congregation formed in 1859.

MONTGOMERY COUNTY

Montgomery County's historic faiths are reflected in today's leading groups: Christian Church or Church of Christ, United Methodist, and American Baptist. The beautiful county seat, Crawfordsville, Union Township, the "Athens of Indiana," was home to General Lew Wallace, author of *Ben-Hur*. His unique study and library (NHL/NRHP), built in 1898, is located at Pike Street and Wallace Avenue adjacent to historic Lane Place (HABSI/NRHP), the Greek Revival-style home of Senator Henry Lane. The following sites reflect the city's rich religious past:

🏛 WABASH COLLEGE, W. Wabash Avenue, a liberal arts college for men, is a pioneer Presbyterian institution founded in 1832, though non-sectarian now. The major campus buildings are arranged around a mall. Among them are historic Caleb Mills House constructed in Federal style in 1836, Forest Hall dating from 1833, and Center Hall built in 1856. The graceful college chapel, built in 1929 in a Georgian Revival style, located on the south end of the mall, is a memorial to the Pioneers of Indiana.

🏛 ★ ST. JOHN'S EPISCOPAL CHURCH, Green Street and Ambrose Whitlock Lane, is the oldest Episcopal church in the state. This simple, well preserved Greek Revival church dates from 1837. Originally located at Water and Market streets, the building was moved to the present site in the winter of 1872–1873. During the move, the apparatus hauling the building was stuck in the mud of the unpaved street from December through March; church services were held inside as usual. NRHP

★ CENTER (WABASH AVENUE) PRESBYTERIAN CHURCH, S. Washington Street and W. Wabash Avenue, red brick Gothic Revival church dates from 1880, built for congregation originating in 1824.

★ FIRST CHRISTIAN CHURCH, W. Wabash Avenue and S. Walnut Street, a splendid Romanesque Revival red brick structure built in 1888, the congregation dates from 1826.

★ BETHEL AFRICAN METHODIST EPISCOPAL CHURCH, W. North between Grand and Walnut streets, a simple, white carpenter-built structure dating from 1890.

OTHER SITES IN MONTGOMERY COUNTY:

★ GRAVELLY RUN FRIENDS CHURCH, CR 150N between 500E and 600E, Franklin Township, Greek Revival structure built in 1880, congregation organized around 1830.

★ WAVELAND CHRISTIAN CHURCH, Main and Jackson streets, Waveland, Brown Township, red brick Gothic Revival structure dating from 1890.

★ WAVELAND COMMUNITY BUILDING, E. Main and Vine Street, formerly Waveland Methodist Church, Waveland, Brown Township, brick Romanesque Revival edifice constructed in 1869.

★ BROWN'S VALLEY CHRISTIAN CHURCH, Washington and Maple streets, Brown's Valley, Brown Township, red brick Romanesque Revival church dating from 1899.

OWEN COUNTY

Owen County's leading attractions are McCormick's Creek State Park and the Owen-Putnam State Forest. Its religious heritage is carried on through these leading religious groups: American Baptists, United Methodists, and Christian Church or Church of Christ. The county seat, Spencer, Washington Township, is noted as the birthplace of Helen Belles Macmillan, mother of British Prime Minister Harold Macmillan (1894–1986). Reminders of the town's rich past are preserved through these fine limestone churches:

★ FIRST UNITED METHODIST CHURCH, W. Morgan and S. Montgomery streets, congregation organized in 1823, the imposing limestone Gothic Revival building dates from 1892–1895.

Saint John's Episcopal Church, Crawfordsville, Montgomery County

★ SPENCER PRESBYTERIAN CHURCH, N. Main and E. North streets, limestone English Gothic Revival building erected 1870, burned 1877, and rebuilt 1879. Congregation formed in 1870.

★ FIRST CHRISTIAN CHURCH, W. Market and S. Montgomery streets, Gothic Revival limestone structure built in 1896, congregation organized in 1833.

★ FIRST BAPTIST CHURCH, E. Morgan and N. Washington streets, congregation started in 1871, imposing limestone Romanesque Revival building erected in 1907.

OTHER SITES IN OWEN COUNTY:

GOSPORT UNITED METHODIST CHURCH, W. North and N. Seventh streets, Gosport, Wayne Township, red brick Gothic Revival building dates from 1880, congregation formed in 1849.

BETHANY PRESBYTERIAN CHURCH, U.S. 231 and CR 700N, north of Carp, Montgomery Township, carpenter built church of congregation founded in 1820.

PARKE COUNTY

Parke County is famed for its thirty-three covered bridges—the state's largest concentration of these fine monuments from the past— and the reason for the annual Covered Bridge Festival. The county is also home to two leading state parks, Turkey Run and Shades. Today's major religious groups are Christian Church or Church of Christ, United Methodist, and American Baptist. These churches can be found around the county:

★ MEMORIAL PRESBYTERIAN CHURCH, S. Market Street, on the courthouse square, Rockville, Adams Township, (the county seat), the red brick Romanesque Revival church was built in 1891 for congregation founded in 1832.

FIRST UNITED METHODIST CHURCH, W. York and N. Market streets, Rockville, Adams Township, red brick English Gothic Revival structure built in 1910, congregation established 1837.

BILLIE CREEK VILLAGE, on U.S. 36 one mile east of Rockville, Adams Township, is a turn-of-the-century village, farmstead, and living museum with three covered bridges and thirty historic buildings. Among the village buildings is the former St. Joseph Catholic Church, moved from its site in downtown Rockville. This gable-front structure was built in 1886; its interior is maintained as a Catholic church of the early twentieth century and is used for non-denominational services and weddings. The other church building is the former Union Baptist Church of Hollandsburg, a white frame Greek Revival structure built in 1859 and moved to the village from Hollandsburg in Union Township.

ELSEWHERE IN PARKE COUNTY:

★ BLOOMINGDALE FRIENDS MEETING, S. School Street and CR 50W, Bloomingdale, Penn Township, excellent white frame vernacular style church built in 1865, Friends formed this congregation in 1827.

HARMONY CHURCH OF CHRIST, U.S. 36 and CR 325W (Mecca Road), Reserve Township, a simple well preserved carpenter built structure dating from 1889, the year of the congregation's founding.

INDEPENDENT BIBLE CHURCH, Jefferson Street near Adams Street, Montezuma, Reserve Township, red brick Gothic Revival church built in 1895 for Methodist Episcopal congregation dating from 1823.

OLD LOG CHURCH, Turkey Run State Park, Howard Township, a log structure built in 1871 on Brisley Ridge in Sugar Creek Township, later abandoned, and was moved to the park in 1923. The church is used for interdenominational religious services each Sunday during the summer.

★ LIBERTY REGULAR BAPTIST CHURCH, CR 40E , northeast of Rosedale, Florida Township, carpenter built house of worship dating from 1852.

PUTNAM COUNTY

Putnam County's leading religious groups today are American Baptists, United Methodists, and Christian Church or Church of Christ. The county is home to DePauw University in Greencastle, the state's historic Methodist institution of higher learning. Founded as Indiana Asbury College in 1837, it acquired its present name in 1884 to honor major donor, Washington DePauw, a New Albany businessman. A visit to these historic sites at DePauw also allows for a pleasant stroll around the scenic campus:

🏛 OLD BETHEL CHURCH, Locust and Seminary streets, DePauw University, is Indiana's first Methodist church. Built in 1807 by Nathan Robertson and his sons on a farm near Charlestown (see Southeast Region—Clark County), it is the place of the first Methodist baptism in Indiana and in its yard the state's first Methodist camp meeting took place. In 1953, the log church was moved to DePauw and restored.

GOBIN MEMORIAL UNITED METHODIST CHURCH, Locust and Seminary streets (next to Old Bethel), resulted from the merger in 1924 of the two historic Methodist churches in Greencastle, College Avenue Church and Locust Avenue Church. It is a striking Neo-Gothic structure completed in 1929 and has fine stained-glass windows depicting the Triumphant Christ, Bishop Francis Asbury, John Wesley, and the Sermon on the Mount.

🏛 In front of the University's Roy West Library stands a large granite shaft marking the GRAVES OF BISHOP ROBERT RICHFORD ROBERTS AND HIS WIFE ELIZABETH OLDHAM ROBERTS. Born in Maryland in 1778, Roberts served as itinerant preacher and minister of Light Street Church in Baltimore. Chosen bishop for the Western Conference in 1816, he was the first Methodist bishop to reside west of the Alleghenies and in Indiana at his farm in Lawrence County until his death in 1843. Elizabeth Roberts was the first Methodist bishop's wife. The grave is a United Methodist Historic Site.

🏛 EAST COLLEGE, in the heart of DePauw's campus, is a splendid red brick Victorian Gothic structure serving as the principal campus building since its dedication in 1871. Meharry Hall on the second floor has been the place for college worship and convocations through the decades. NRHP

OTHER SITES IN GREENCASTLE, THE COUNTY SEAT:

★ ST. PAUL CATHOLIC CHURCH, Washington Street between College and Spring streets, red brick Victorian Romanesque building dates from 1852 with additions made later, used by a Presbyterian congregation to 1866. Catholic parish was started in 1848.

★ FIRST CHRISTIAN CHURCH, Indiana and Poplar streets, fine Victorian Romanesque building constructed in 1890, congregation was established in 1830.

★ FIRST SOUTHERN BAPTIST CHURCH, S. Crown and Apple streets, frame Gothic Revival church built in 1850, used originally by Catholic parish until 1866 and for nearly a century by African Methodist Episcopal congregation before Baptists acquired it in recent years. Building was moved from present site of DePauw University Administration building in 1916.

OTHER SITES IN PUTNAM COUNTY:

★ PUTNAMVILLE UNITED METHODIST CHURCH, Main Cross Street and U.S. 40, Putnamville, Warren Township, Greek Revival structure built in 1834 for a Presbyterian congregation. Methodist congregation organized in 1829 purchased Presbyterian Church in 1860. NRHP

★ ETERNAL GRACE BAPTIST CHURCH, CR 675E and 900N, New Maysville, Jackson Township, Greek Revival structure built around 1850 with Gothic Revival addition.

★ Former UNIVERSALIST CHURCH, U.S. 231 between CR 1000N and 1100N, Franklin Township, red brick Italianate building dating from 1871, congregation relocated here after earlier founding in Russell Township.

★ UNION CHAPEL UNITED METHODIST CHURCH, U.S. 36 and CR 600W, near Morton, Clinton Township, painted-brick Victorian Romanesque building dates from 1896, with surrounding cemetery. Congregation was founded in the 1840s.

East College, DePauw University, Greencastle, Putnam County

★ BRICK CHAPEL UNITED METHODIST CHURCH, U.S. 231 and CR 350N, Monroe, Monroe Township, begun in 1823, known as Montgomery Chapel until 1891, present impressive red brick Romanesque Revival church dates from 1872.

★ CHRISTIAN CHURCH, Main and Hendricks streets, Fillmore, Marion Township, fine red brick Gothic Revival church built in 1910, congregation organized in 1854.

★ Former OTTER CREEK BAPTIST CHURCH, CR 900W and 250S, Madison Township, Italianate style structure built in 1889, congregation organized in Jackson Township, Parke County in 1853 and relocated to present church in 1889.

★ REELSVILLE UNITED METHODIST CHURCH, CR 625W and 700S, Reelsville, Washington Township, Gothic Revival frame style built in 1893; congregation organized in 1889.

SULLIVAN COUNTY

Sullivan County residents enjoy scenic views of the Wabash River on the county's western border, and the county is home to part of Shakamak State Park. The county's religious past is reflected in today's strong presence of American Baptists, United Methodists, and Christian Church or Church of Christ. Within the county, the following religious sites can be found:

🏛 OLD COLLEGE HALL, near SR 63, Merom, Gill Township, an imposing Victorian Romanesque building, dating from 1862, housed a preparatory school, UNION CHRISTIAN COLLEGE, founded by "New Light" Christians and operated from 1859 to 1924. Currently under ownership of the Indiana-Kentucky Synod of the United Church of Christ, Old College Hall and surrounding buildings serve as the synod's conference and retreat center. NRHP

HISTORICAL MARKER, Merom Town Park, Merom, Gill Township, park overlooks the Wabash from a bluff. The marker describes the park as the site of MEROM BLUFF CHAUTAUQUA from 1905 to 1936. Prominent Chautauqua speakers of the era appeared here including evangelist Billy Sunday.

ELSEWHERE IN SULLIVAN COUNTY:

FIRST PRESBYTERIAN CHURCH, Beech and N. Main streets, Sullivan, Hamilton Township, the county seat; congregation was founded in 1859. The present building is a red brick Gothic Revival gem built in 1908.

FIRST UNITED METHODIST CHURCH, Beech and N. Court streets, Sullivan, Hamilton Township, red brick Gothic Revival building begun in 1889, congregation established in 1847.

SHAKER PRAIRIE CHRISTIAN CHURCH, CR 300W and 1050S, Haddon Township,

Old College Hall, Merom, Sullivan County

the old part of building dates from 1917, the adjacent Shepherd Cemetery dates from 1820. The church site is on land once owned by Shaker Community.

BETHEL UNITED METHODIST CHURCH, SR 48, Hymera, Jackson Township, is an excellent yellow brick Gothic Revival building dating from 1913, congregation started in 1835.

TAYLOR MEMORIAL PRAYER CHAPEL, U.S. 41, Farmersburg, Curry Township, is a small nondenominational place of worship built of cinder blocks in 1956. Travelers are welcome to stop here for prayer. A local minister and his wife created this memorial to the former's brother and sister who were killed in an auto accident.

TIPPECANOE COUNTY

The area that is now Tippecanoe County attracted the interest of early French traders and explorers who established historic Fort Ouiatenon. The county is also location of the Tippecanoe Battlefield (NHL/NRHP) where General William Henry Harrison defeated an Indian Confederation in 1811. Today's center of population is Lafayette and adjacent West Lafayette, the home of Purdue University. The county's leading religious groups are Catholics, United Methodists, and Presbyterians. These groups have produced some of these exceptional sites:

★ FORT OUIATENON HISTORICAL PARK, South River Road, West Lafayette, located on the banks of the Wabash River, recalls the first European settlement in the state. In 1717, the French established a military and trading post among the Wea Indians and introduced Catholicism to the area. When local physician, Richard B. Weatherill, developed the site in 1928, it was thought to be the precise location of the original fort. The actual site, however, is located on private property some distance away and is not now accessible to visitors. NRHP/NT

At Lafayette, Fairfield Township, the county seat, the historic congregations of the major faiths remain at their downtown locations. With spires piercing the sky, the churches preserve some of the city's historic skyline:

🏛 ★ ST. JOHN EPISCOPAL CHURCH, Ferry and N. Sixth streets, the city's oldest church building, this beautiful Gothic Revival structure was built in 1851 according to design of William Tinsley, architect of Indianapolis's Christ Church. Historic parish was formed in 1837. NRHP

★ UNITARIAN-UNIVERSALIST CHURCH, S. Seventh and Alabama streets, Italianate structure built in 1866–1867 for Temple Israel, formed in 1849 as the second Jewish congregation in the state. Only Fort Wayne's Achduth Vesholom congregation, formed in 1848, is older. NRHP

★ ST. JAMES LUTHERAN CHURCH, Cincinnati at N. Eighth streets, yellow brick Gothic Revival building dates from 1872, congregation started in 1850.

★ TRINITY UNITED METHODIST CHURCH, North and N. Sixth streets, red brick Gothic Revival building dates from 1869, the congregation was formed in the same year.

★ FIRST BAPTIST CHURCH, North and N. Seventh streets, is an elegant and imposing red brick Renaissance Revival monument dating from 1868–1872, congregation organized in early 1830s.

★ ST. BONIFACE CATHOLIC CHURCH, N. Ninth and North streets, red brick Romanesque Revival structure built in 1875; this congregation founded for German Catholics dates from 1865.

★ CENTRAL PRESBYTERIAN CHURCH, Columbia and N. Seventh streets, this limestone Richardsonian Romanesque building resembling a fortress was built in 1894; the congregation dates from 1828.

★ ST. MARY OF THE IMMACULATE CONCEPTION CATHEDRAL, Columbia and N. Eleventh streets, perma stone Gothic Revival structure dating from 1864, has impressive location on hill overlooking the city, its lofty spire visible for miles. The city's first Catholic parish dates from 1842. As a cathedral, it is the official church of the Catholic bishop of the Lafayette diocese.

★ BROWN STREET UNITED METHODIST CHURCH, Brown and N. Ninth streets, founded as German Methodist Episcopal Church in 1851, the red brick Gothic Revival structure was built in 1885.

★ ST. LAWRENCE CATHOLIC CHURCH, Meharry and N. Nineteenth streets, brick Renaissance Revival church built in 1915, congregation organized in 1895.

★ PENTECOSTAL CHURCH OF GOD, Elizabeth and N. Eleventh streets, formerly German Evangelical Church, red brick Gothic Revival building dates from 1905.

★ ST. ANN CATHOLIC CHURCH, Wabash Avenue and Green Street, red brick Gothic Revival church dates from 1893, parish founded in 1870.

★ STIDHAM MEMORIAL PRESBYTERIAN CHURCH, 375 Elston Road, just west of U.S. 231 South, is an excellent Arts and Crafts style church built in 1920 for congregation organized in 1912. Church is similar in style to Stidham United Methodist Church in Union Township (below).

OTHER SITES IN TIPPECANOE COUNTY:

★ FARMERS INSTITUTE ACADEMY (Friends), CR 660S near 475W, Union Township, gable-front Greek Revival structure dates from 1851, for Farmers Institute Monthly Meeting of Friends dating from 1828. NRHP

★ BATTLEFIELD CHAPEL, Battle Ground, Tippecanoe Township, was a Methodist chapel built in gable-front style in 1820s at the Tippecanoe Battlefield (NHL). The battle-

First Baptist Church, Lafayette, Tippecanoe County

ground was the location of Methodist camp meetings beginning in 1875. The Northwest Indiana Methodist Conference operated a college, Battle Ground Institute, here from 1858 to 1876. NT

★ BATTLE GROUND UNITED METHODIST CHURCH, Tipton and Winans streets, Battle Ground, Tippecanoe Township, Gothic Revival building dates from 1919 for congregation formed in 1857.

★ MONTMORENCI BAPTIST CHURCH, Main Street (U.S. 231) and U.S. 52, Montmorenci, Shelby Township, founded as United Brethren Church in 1909, red brick Colonial Revival building dates from 1920.

★ MEMORIAL PRESBYTERIAN CHURCH, Walnut Street (SR 38) and Ricks Drive, Dayton, Sheffield Township, a fine Romanesque Revival church built in 1899 for congregation formed in 1834.

★ CALVARY CHAPEL, SR 25 near CR 300S, Shadeland, Union Township, a graceful red brick Gothic Revival structure built in 1870.

★ STIDHAM UNITED METHODIST CHURCH, CR 175W and 500S, Union Township, an exceptionally charming Arts and Crafts style church built in 1915 at the time of its founding and named for founding donor, Jasper Stidham.

★ ROMNEY PRESBYTERIAN CHURCH, Main (U.S. 231) and Elm streets, Romney, Randolph Township, this excellent brick Arts and Crafts style building dates from 1914, congregation organized in 1845.

★ ROMNEY UNITED METHODIST CHURCH, High Street near Main Street, Romney, Randolph Township, red brick Gothic Revival church with graceful spire built in 1875, congregation began in 1830.

WAYSIDE CHAPEL, 8005 SR 52 West near CR 800N, Shelby Township, a small chapel located on a busy highway as a place for travellers to stop and pray. Founded by the Lafayette Christian Reformed Church in 1966, the chapel is similar to others throughout the country sponsored by the Christian Reformed denomination.

VERMILLION COUNTY

United Methodists, Catholics, and American Baptists are the leading religious bodies in Vermillion County, which is home to the Ernie Pyle Birthplace State Historic Site at Dana, the area's principal historic attraction. The county seat is Newport, but its largest municipality, Clinton, is the location of a group of historic congregations representing the major faiths:

FIRST CHRISTIAN CHURCH, S. 7th and Blackman streets, congregation organized in 1888, red brick Classical Revival structure built in 1913.

SACRED HEART CATHOLIC CHURCH, Nebeker and S. 6th streets, parish was formed in 1891, red brick Romanesque Revival church was built in 1909 to resemble the Cathedral of Thurles, Ireland.

FIRST BAPTIST CHURCH, S. 5th and Walnut streets, its home is a twentieth-century Classical Revival building dating from 1909, year of congregation's founding.

UNITED PRESBYTERIAN CHURCH, Mulberry and S. 3rd streets, fine red brick Romanesque Revival structure built in 1896 for congregation started in 1831.

FIRST UNITED METHODIST CHURCH, Blackman and S. 4th streets, handsome twentieth-century brick Romanesque Revival church built in 1915, congregation established in 1831.

OTHER SITES IN VERMILLION COUNTY:

SALEM UNITED METHODIST CHURCH, SR 63 and CR 1050S, Helt Township, about five miles north of Clinton, an attractive red brick Gothic Revival church built in 1878 for congregation founded in 1828. NRHP

PERRYVILLE UNITED METHODIST CHURCH, Washington and Liberty streets, Perryville, Highland Township, congregation established in 1821, occupies stucco Gothic Revival building.

DANA UNITED METHODIST CHURCH, Linden Street and Redwood Avenue, Dana, Helt Township, fine red brick Gothic Revival building constructed in 1906, congregation dates from 1877.

VIGO COUNTY

Vigo County's largest religious groups are Catholics, United Methodists, and the Christian Church or Church of Christ. Terre Haute, Harrison Township, the county seat and major population center, is home of Indiana State University and Rose-Hulman Institute of Technology. Socialist presidential candidate Eugene V. Debs's house (NHL/NRHP) and songwriter Paul Dresser's birthplace (NRHP) are the city's leading historic buildings. Max Ehrmann, lawyer-poet and author of "Desiderata" and "A Prayer," was a lifelong resident. Terre Haute is also home to these historic churches:

★ ALLEN CHAPEL AFRICAN METHODIST EPISCOPAL CHURCH, 3rd (U.S. 41) and Crawford streets, built in 1870, rebuilt in 1913 in yellow brick Gothic Revival style, congregation formed in 1839. NRHP

★ IMMANUEL EVANGELICAL LUTHERAN CHURCH, 635 Poplar Street, across from the Vigo County Library, congregation founded in 1858; present red brick Gothic Revival church, exceptionally graceful in appearance, was built in 1885.

★ First Congregational Church, 630 E. Ohio Street, light brick Gothic Revival structure built in 1902, congregation organized in 1834, the state's first Congregationalist church.

★ St. Joseph Catholic Church, 115 Fifth Street, serves as Catholic Campus Center for Indiana State University. The church building is a red brick Romanesque Revival structure built in 1910, parish organized in 1842.

★ St. Stephen Episcopal Church, 7th and Eagle streets, limestone Gothic Revival building erected in 1862 and remodeled in 1906, the parish's first church was erected in 1845.

★ Centenary United Methodist Church, 7th and Eagle streets, opposite St. Stephen Episcopal Church, limestone Romanesque Revival building dates from 1902, congregation organized in 1866.

★ St. Benedict Catholic Church, Ninth and Ohio streets, red brick Romanesque Revival edifice of monumental quality built in 1896 with substantial support of German-born business leader Herman Hulman; congregation was formed for German Catholics in 1865.

★ United Hebrew Congregation, 540 S. Sixth Street, founded in 1891 as Temple Israel, its stately limestone Classical Revival style building dates from 1911. The building is Indiana's oldest Jewish house of worship in continuous use.

★ Emmanuel Temple Apostolic Church, Kent Avenue and Chestnut Street, former Kent Avenue congregation of the Evangelical Association founded in 1881, present Tudor Gothic building dates from 1911.

★ First United Brethren Church, Chestnut and 14th streets, Classical Revival structure dates from 1918, congregation founded in 1865.

Central Presbyterian Church, N. 7th and Larry Bird streets, congregation organized in 1828, its home is a fine red brick Romanesque Revival church built in 1863 and enlarged in 1882.

★ Highland Lawn Cemetery Chapel, 4520 Wabash Avenue (U.S. 40), is an excellent stone Richardsonian Romanesque Revival structure built in 1890. Max Ehrmann is buried in cemetery that is listed on NRHP.

Elsewhere in Vigo County:

🏛 ★ St. Mary-of-the-Woods, St. Mary's Road, west of U.S. 150, Sugar Creek Township, is home to the General Administration of the Sisters of Providence, the first Catholic women's religious order established in the state. French émigré sisters led by Mother Theodore Guerin established convent here in 1840. The Sisters of Providence have historically conducted parochial and high schools in the region. At the

United Hebrew Congregation, Terre Haute, Vigo County

site, they sponsor a liberal arts college for women, St. Mary-of-the-Woods College. "The Woods" includes some eighteen outstanding buildings including the Renaissance Revival CHURCH OF THE IMMACULATE CONCEPTION, built in 1886–1892 according to D. A. Bohlen design, Providence Hall constructed in 1889, and the college's main building, Le Fer Hall, built in 1921–1923.

★ ST. MARY-OF-THE-WOODS CATHOLIC CHURCH, Miami Road, Sugar Creek Township, west of the above, is the parish church for the local village founded in 1837, the perma stone Gothic Revival structure dates from 1867.

★ BETHANY UNITED CHURCH OF CHRIST, Miller Avenue and Church Street, West Terre Haute, Sugar Creek Township, organized in 1885 as Congregational church, present red brick Gothic Revival structure erected in 1909.

★ HISTORICAL MARKER, Hunt Street and Debney Avenue, near Seelyville, Lost Creek Township, is the site of LOST CREEK AFRICAN METHODIST EPISCOPAL CHURCH, which existed from 1840 to 1949. It was a stop on the Underground Railroad that brought escaped slaves northward to Canada before the Civil War. Official AME Church Historic Site.

★ FIRST PRAIRIE CREEK BAPTIST CHURCH, 157th Street and SR 63, Prairie Creek Township, a Greek Revival gem dating from 1840 with cemetery.

GIBAULT SCHOOL FOR BOYS, 6301 S. U.S. 41, Allendale, Honey Creek Township, is a Catholic institution serving adolescents with emotional, situational, or behavioral problems. Founded in 1921 and supported by the Knights of Columbus of Indiana, the school occupies former estate of Terre Haute distiller, Fred B. Smith, whose mansion built in Prairie School style in 1910 is original campus building.

WARREN COUNTY

Warren County's leading religious groups are United Methodists, Christian Church or Church of Christ, and Presbyterian. The county seat at Williamsport, Washington Township, is home to these fine church buildings:

WILLIAMSPORT UNITED METHODIST CHURCH, Monroe Street, stone Gothic Revival structure erected in 1894–1895, congregation dates from 1833.

Former PRESBYTERIAN CHURCH, Fall Street, handsome stucco Gothic Revival building constructed in 1890 for congregation formed in 1850. Congregation has merged with Presbyterian church in Attica, Fountain County, to form Attica-Williamsport Presbyterian Church.

Church of the Immaculate Conception, Saint Mary-of-the-Woods, Vigo County

ALSO SEE:

TRINITY PRESBYTERIAN CHURCH, Third and Clinton streets, West Lebanon, Pike Township, red brick Romanesque Revival structure built in 1898, congregation was organized in 1859.

Central Region

Boone County

In Boone County, named for frontiersman Daniel Boone, the leading religious groups today are Catholic, United Methodist, and Christian Church or Church of Christ. Historic churches are located across the county including those at Lebanon, Center Township, the county seat:

★ FIRST BAPTIST CHURCH, E. Washington and N. East streets, this imposing Georgian Revival building dates from 1912, congregation was formed in 1873.

★ INDIANA METHODIST CHILDREN'S HOME, 515 Camp Street, established in 1919 by the Northwest Indiana Conference of the Methodist Episcopal Church, the Prairie Style building dates from 1927.

★ FIRST PRESBYTERIAN CHURCH, E. Main and S. East streets, red brick Gothic Revival church built in 1873, congregation organized in 1840.

OTHER SITES IN BOONE COUNTY:

★ TRINITY CHAPEL, U.S. 52 at CR 450N, Washington Township, frame Gothic Revival Eastlake style structure built around 1885.

★ SUGAR PLAIN FRIENDS CHURCH, SR 47 and CR 900W, west of Thorntown, Sugar Creek Township, excellent carpenter built structure dating from 1893 with historic cemetery.

★ THORNTOWN PRESBYTERIAN CHURCH, Main and S. West streets, Thorntown, Sugar Creek Township, buff brick Gothic Revival building dates from 1924, congregation organized in 1830.

★ FRANCIS NIEDLINGER POST #79, American Legion, W. Walnut and N. Fourth streets, Zionsville, Eagle Township, Romanesque Revival structure built for Christian Union Church in 1870, home of Boone Post Grand Army of the Republic, 1898–1926. Legion Post since 1919.

★ Former FIRST BAPTIST CHURCH, N. Main and Poplar streets, Zionsville, Eagle Township, frame Queen Anne style structure dating from 1894, built for the local Methodist congregation organized in 1828.

★ JAMESTOWN UNITED METHODIST CHURCH, S. High and Jefferson streets, Jamestown,

Jackson Township, Romanesque Revival building dates from 1870–1871, congregation established in 1833.

CLINTON COUNTY

Clinton County's rolling landscape is dotted with farms while industries are located at the county seat, Frankfort. Religious groups now prominent in the county are United Methodist, Christian Church or Church of Christ, and American Baptist. Frankfort, Center Township, has the largest group of fine church buildings:

FIRST CHRISTIAN CHURCH, W. Walnut and Columbia streets, red brick Romanesque Revival church built in 1892, congregation organized in 1830.

FIRST PRESBYTERIAN CHURCH, W. Clinton Street, congregation founded in 1861, red brick Romanesque Revival building dates from 1875–1876 with later additions.

FIRST BAPTIST CHURCH, S. Columbia and W. Wabash streets, congregation organized in 1880, twentieth-century Romanesque Revival church was built in 1913.

HOPE UNITED METHODIST CHURCH, E. Clinton Street between Jackson and Sycamore, founded as First Brethren Church, this imposing twentieth-century Classical Revival building dates from 1925.

ELSEWHERE IN CLINTON COUNTY:

MULBERRY UNITED METHODIST CHURCH, Jefferson Road and Perrin Street, Mulberry, Madison Township, excellent red brick Gothic Revival house of worship built in 1901.

TRINITY UNITED CHURCH OF CHRIST, Jackson (SR 38) and Main streets, Mulberry, Madison Township, founded as Trinity Reformed Church in 1859, the fine red brick Romanesque Revival structure dates from 1895.

MULBERRY BAPTIST CHURCH, Glick Street near Jackson (SR 38), Mulberry, Madison Township, red brick structure with Gothic and Romanesque elements built in 1894 for Zion Evangelical Lutheran Church, a congregation formed in 1867.

COLFAX UNITED METHODIST CHURCH, N. Oakland and W. Jefferson streets, Colfax, Perry Township, a fine dark brick twentieth-century Gothic Revival structure built in 1924, congregation founded in 1840.

COLFAX CHRISTIAN CHURCH, S. Clark Street, Colfax, Perry Township, is an imposing dark brick twentieth-century Gothic Revival structure built in 1912, rose windows enchance its distinctive character.

PLEASANT HILL PRESBYTERIAN CHURCH, U.S. 421 and CR 550N, Warren Township, fine, modest red brick Gothic Revival structure built around turn of the century.

ST. LUKE UNITED CHURCH OF CHRIST, U.S. 421 north of Wildcat Creek, Michigan Township, white frame carpenter-built structure, congregation formed in 1871.

MICHIGANTOWN CHRISTIAN CHURCH, Wabash and 2nd streets, Michigan Township, congregation founded in 1872, red brick Romanesque Revival edifice built in 1911.

KIRKLIN PRESBYTERIAN CHURCH, N. Main Street, Kirklin, Kirklin Township, red brick Romanesque Revival structure dates from 1892, congregation formed in 1867.

HAMILTON COUNTY

Hamilton County, once largely agricultural, has become in recent decades a suburban residential area within greater Indianapolis. Today's leading religious groups in the county are Catholic, United Methodist, and Christian Church or Church of Christ. Noblesville, the county seat, is home to the following historic church buildings:

★ THE ADLER BUILDING, S. 9th and Maple streets, commercial offices housed in a magnificent red brick Gothic Revival complex built in 1897 for First Christian Church, congregation formed in 1834.

★ FIRST PRESBYTERIAN CHURCH, Conner and S. 12th streets, fine red brick Romanesque Revival building dating from 1893, congregation formed in 1848.

ELSEWHERE IN HAMILTON COUNTY:

INDIANA ACADEMY, SR 19, north of Cicero, Jackson Township, founded as Boggstown Manual Training Academy. Moved to present site and renamed in 1919, now a secondary school of the Seventh Day Adventist Church.

★ UNION BIBLE SEMINARY, 415 S. Union Street, Westfield, Washington Township, was founded as Union High School, a Friends school operating from 1861 to the 1890s. In 1911 it was purchased for Union Bible Seminary, an interdenominational holiness school.

CHRIST COMMUNITY CHURCH, Lamong Road and 206th Street, Washington Township, formerly Lamong Friends Meeting, is described as vernacular building dating from 1840, this meeting house is typical of the worship places of this Quaker-settled township.

★ ROBERTS CHAPEL, E. 276th Street just east of U.S. 31, Jackson Township, originally established as a Wesleyan congregation by black settlers from North Carolina, gable-front structure built about 1861, congregation dates from 1838.

★ FIRST CHRISTIAN CHURCH, E. Main Street and Broadway, Atlanta, Jackson Township, a fine yellow brick twentieth-century Gothic Revival building dating from 1909, congregation dates from 1842.

★ ARCADIA CHRISTIAN CHURCH, S. Olive and W. South streets, Arcadia, Jackson Township, pristine red brick Romanesque Revival building dating from 1896, congregation founded in 1869.

★ BETHEL LUTHERAN CHURCH, W. Jackson Street at Washington Avenue, Cicero, Jackson Township, red brick twentieth-century Gothic Revival church built in 1930, congregation formed in 1856.

★ FIRST UNITED METHODIST CHURCH, E. 2nd and S. Adams streets, Sheridan, Adams Township, dark brick, twentieth-century Gothic Revival structure built in 1917, congregation dates from 1875.

HANCOCK COUNTY

Hancock County's leading religious bodies today are United Methodist, Catholic, and Christian Church or Church of Christ. The county seat, Greenfield, Center Township, is noted as the birthplace of Hoosier poet, James Whitcomb Riley, and location of his boyhood home (NRHP). These historic congregations date from Riley's lifetime:

★ CHRISTIAN CHURCH, N. East and E. North streets, an excellent Victorian Romanesque edifice built in 1895 for the city's historic Christian congregation.

★ BRADLEY UNITED METHODIST CHURCH, W. Main and N. Pennsylvania streets, an imposing limestone Richardsonian Romanesque building dating from 1902; congregation founded about 1830.

★ FIRST PRESBYTERIAN CHURCH, S. Pennsylvania and W. South streets, red brick Victorian Romanesque church built in 1906, congregation organized in 1855.

ELSEWHERE IN HANCOCK COUNTY:

★ UNITED METHODIST CHURCH, Main (SR 109) and F streets, Wilkinson, Brown Township, a frame late Gothic Revival building dating from 1911, congregation established in 1840.

★ SUGAR GROVE UNITED METHODIST CHURCH, CR 900N and 550E, Green Township, founded as United Brethren congregation in 1885, Gothic Revival building dates from 1919–1920.

★ EDEN UNITED METHODIST CHURCH, Eden Road (CR 840N) just east of SR 9, Eden, Green Township, a Victorian Gothic Revival church in excellent condition built in

1904, congregation dates from 1834. Site of Thomas Fuqua log cabin built in 1831, the first structure built in Hancock County.

★ UNITED METHODIST CHURCH, SR 67 and McCord Street, McCordsville, Vernon Township, splendid Tudor Gothic building constructed in 1921 for a congregation dating from 1854.

★ UNITED METHODIST CHURCH, 125 E. Staat Street, Fortville, Vernon Township, red brick late Gothic Revival church dating from 1901, congregation formed in 1856.

★ ST. THOMAS THE APOSTLE CATHOLIC CHURCH, Maple and Garden streets, Fortville, Vernon Township, small Romanesque Revival church built in 1916 for parish originating in 1869.

★ CURRY'S CHAPEL UNITED METHODIST CHURCH, CR 375E between 300N and 400N, Center Township, Late Gothic Revival structure built in 1900, congregation organized in 1834.

★ UNITED METHODIST CHURCH, Mill Street, New Palestine, Sugar Creek Township, Romanesque Revival church built in 1901, congregation formed in 1830.

HENDRICKS COUNTY

Hendricks County relates closely to greater Indianapolis as a suburban residential area. The county's leading religious bodies are United Methodist and Christian Church or Church of Christ. Its historic rural and small-town character is maintained with the following fine churches:

★ FIRST PRESBYTERIAN CHURCH, N. Jefferson and W. Clinton streets, Danville, the county seat, Center Township, red brick Queen Anne style built in 1884, congregation organized in 1832.

★ DANVILLE CHRISTIAN CHURCH, E. Main and Cross streets, Danville, an imposing Neo-Classical building dating from 1914 at a prominent downtown location, congregation organized in 1844.

★ GOOD SHEPHERD LUTHERAN CHURCH, 204 E. Main Street, Brownsburg, Lincoln Township, is the downtown area's most prominent church building, a red brick Gothic Revival structure built in 1923 for Methodist congregation dating from 1828.

★ SHILOH UNITED METHODIST CHURCH, CR 1050E just south of 100N, Washington Township, is the oldest congregation in the county, present building dates from 1902, congregation founded in 1823.

★ FIRST BAPTIST CHURCH, South Street and Tudor Road, Stilesville, Franklin Township, excellent red brick Gothic Revival church built in 1881, congregation founded in 1830s.

★ Former ST. MARK'S EPISCOPAL CHURCH, S. Center and Fremont streets, Plainfield, Guilford Township, a lovely, brick Gothic Revival church built in 1891 for Methodist Episcopal congregation. St. Mark's Episcopal parish, dating from 1953, used building from 1987 to 1994. St. Mark's rector, Rev. Jacqueline Means, was the first woman ordained an Episcopal priest.

★ INDIANA BOYS SCHOOL CHAPEL, on the Indiana Boys School campus, west of Plainfield on U.S. 40, Guilford Township, a fine Neo-Classical structure built in 1911.

HISTORICAL MARKER, Main Street near S. East Street, Plainfield, Guilford Township, in front of Plainfield Friends Meeting, describes the WESTERN FRIENDS MEETING established here in 1858. It was the site of Friends Central Academy from 1881 to 1919. The present Friends Meeting was erected in 1914 and has had several additions.

ISLAMIC CENTER OF NORTH AMERICA, CR 750E (Old SR 267) near Hadley Road, south of Plainfield, Guilford Township, built in 1981–1982 in a contemporary Islamic style, is visible to drivers on Interstate 70. The Center, a national religious and educational institution, was formed in 1963 as the Muslim Students Association at the University of Illinois at Urbana. It was relocated to current site because of central location. This is the principal Islamic site in Indiana.

JOHNSON COUNTY

Johnson County combines the new and the old with the growing suburban residential areas adjacent to Indianapolis and in many well preserved historic churches. The county's leading religious groups are Catholic, United Methodist, and those adhering to Christian Church or Church of Christ. The following sites are located in Franklin, the county seat:

🏛 FRANKLIN COLLEGE, E. Monroe Street, this coeducational liberal arts college is Indiana's historic Baptist institution of higher education. Chartered in 1834 as Indiana Baptist Manual Labor Institute, it acquired present name in 1841. Prominent Baptist Jesse Holman Lynch was leader in its founding. (See his home in Southeast Region—Dearborn County.) Old Main Building was built in stages from 1847 to 1888. (NRHP) The college chapel is of modern design.

★ FRANKLIN FIRST BAPTIST CHURCH, E. Jefferson and Home Avenue, congregation organized in 1832, at present site since 1838, where the imposing red brick Romanesque Revival church building was constructed in 1885. Near the Franklin College campus.

Islamic Center of North America, Plainfield, Hendricks County

★ FIRST PRESBYTERIAN CHURCH, E. Madison and N. Water streets, exceptionally graceful red brick Gothic Revival church dates from 1875 for congregation formed in 1824.

★ FRANKLIN GOSPEL ASSEMBLY, E. Madison Street and N. Home Avenue, red brick Gothic Revival church dates from 1868 and rebuilt in 1930 for Methodist congregation formed in 1825.

★ TABERNACLE CHRISTIAN CHURCH, N. Water and King streets, stone Gothic Revival building dates from 1902, congregation formed in 1848.

★ CHRISTIAN CHURCH, E. Madison and Yandes streets, simple Gothic Revival structure built in 1873–1874.

Edinburgh, in Blue River Township, is Johnson County's oldest town and the location of several of the county's historic congregations:

★ FIRST PRESBYTERIAN CHURCH, E. Main Cross Street near Kyle Street, small brick building in Arts and Crafts style dating from 1916, congregation organized in 1864.

★ FIRST CHRISTIAN CHURCH, Walnut and Perry streets, red brick Romanesque Revival church built in 1887, congregation started in 1834. An early pastor of this congregation, Rev. Knowles Shaw, composed the hymn "Bringing in the Sheaves."

★ CHURCH, FOUNDED AS EDINBURGH COLORED BAPTIST CHURCH, Main and Center Cross streets, carpenter-built in 1880–1881 at time of congregation's founding.

★ HOLY TRINITY CATHOLIC CHURCH, Keely Street, is a small red brick Gothic Revival edifice dating from 1883, well positioned on a crest overlooking the town, parish dates from 1851.

EDINBURGH UNITED METHODIST CHURCH, Main and Campbell streets, splendid Gothic Revival structure with Romanesque Revival tower, congregation founded in 1848.

OTHER SITES IN JOHNSON COUNTY:

★ ST. JOSEPH TRADITIONAL CATHOLIC CHURCH AND PRIORY, W. Broadway and Smart Street, Greenwood, Pleasant Township, Romanesque Revival church built about 1890 for Greenwood Christian congregation, formed in 1860.

★ GREENWOOD PRESBYTERIAN CHURCH, W. Main and Brewer streets, Greenwood, Pleasant Township, red brick Romanesque Revival building dates from 1898, congregation began in 1825.

★ PROVIDENCE CHRISTIAN CHURCH, CR 100N west of 400N, Union Township, red brick Romanesque Revival edifice built in 1905.

★ HOPEWELL PRESBYTERIAN CHURCH, SR 144 and CR 100N, Franklin Township, an excellent Romanesque Revival church dating from 1902 for congregation organized in 1831, historical marker notes the site of Hopewell Academy operating here from 1855 to 1889.

★ SECOND MT. PLEASANT BAPTIST CHURCH, CR 150S and 800E, Needham Township, Jacobethan Revival building dates from 1928, congregation organized in 1835.

★ JOLLITY UNITED METHODIST CHURCH, CR 800E near 400S, Blue River Township, Italianate style structure built in 1871, founded as Methodist Protestant congregation in 1830.

★ FIRST CHRISTIAN CHURCH, East Street between Harriman and South streets, Bargersville, White River Township, red brick Romanesque Revival structure built in 1916, congregation formed in 1861.

CHAPEL IN THE MEADOW, OR ITALIAN PRISONER OF WAR CHAPEL, Stone Arch Road, Camp Atterbury, Nineveh Township, is located on this historic military reservation now subdivided for several uses. Site is accessible from U.S. 31, then west on SR 252, and south on CR 200E. The chapel, only eleven by sixteen feet in area and built with surplus material, is the handiwork of Italian prisoners of war held at Camp Atterbury during World War II. The prisoner-artists painted the interior using dyes produced from berries, flower petals, and plants. The chapel was completely restored in 1988 and rededicated in 1989.

MARION COUNTY

As Indiana's capital and largest city, Indianapolis is the location of the state's largest concentration of National Historic Landmarks including the Dentzel Carousel at the Children's Museum, Butler University's Hinkle Fieldhouse, the Benjamin Harrison House, the Indianapolis Motor Speedway, the James Whitcomb Riley House (HABS), and the Madam C. J. Walker Building. The city is likewise home to a rich array of denominational headquarters, church-related institutions of higher education, and distinguished church buildings. The city's leading religious bodies today are Catholic, black Baptist, United Methodist, Christian Church or Church of Christ, and Christian Church (Disciples of Christ).

DENOMINATIONAL HEADQUARTERS:

CHRISTIAN CHURCH (DISCIPLES OF CHRIST) INTERNATIONAL OFFICES, 130 E. Washington Street, relocated to present downtown office building in 1995 from longtime home in buildings of the former campus of Butler University in Irvington. The denomination has been a significant presence in the state since the early nineteenth century.

WESLEYAN CHURCH INTERNATIONAL CENTER, 6060 Castleway Drive West,

Castleton, formerly at Marion, Indiana, moved its international headquarters to present location in 1987. Nearby is the denomination's Wesley Press at 8050 Castleway Drive.

FREE METHODIST CHURCH OF NORTH AMERICA WORLD HEADQUARTERS, 770 N. High School Road, moved from Winona Lake, Indiana to present location in 1990. The denomination originated in 1860 among dissident members of the Methodist Episcopal Church.

PENTECOSTAL ASSEMBLIES OF THE WORLD has its headquarters at 3939 Meadows Drive. The denomination's main office has been located in the city since 1919. Its historic role in the local African American community is linked to Bishop Garfield T. Haywood and his Christ Temple, 430 W. Fall Creek Parkway.

INTERCHURCH CENTER, 1100 W. 42nd Street, houses local and regional offices of several denominations and religious organizations in a building of contemporary design completed in 1967. The complex houses the following offices: the Episcopal Diocese of Indianapolis, the Indiana-Kentucky Synod of the United Church of Christ, the Christian Church (Disciples of Christ) of Indiana, the Indiana Area United Methodist Church, the Indiana Interreligious Commission on Human Equality, the Jewish Community Relations Council, the Presbyterian Church's Synod of Lincoln Trails, the Church Federation of Greater Indianapolis, and the Church World Service.

★ ARCHBISHOP EDWARD O'MEARA CATHOLIC CENTER, 1400 N. Meridian Street, houses offices of the Catholic Archdiocese of Indianapolis in the former Cathedral High School, a Neo-Classical building dating from 1926–1927.

HIGHER EDUCATION WITH RELIGIOUS AFFILIATION OR BACKGROUND:

🏛 CHRISTIAN THEOLOGICAL SEMINARY, 1000 W. 42nd Street, is the theological seminary historically linked to the Christian Church (Disciples of Christ). It was formerly the School of Religion of adjacent Butler University until 1958. New York architect Edward Larrabee Barnes designed this splendid complex of buildings based on Middle Eastern style dating from the time of Christ. Built in stages from the 1960s at a scenic location overlooking the White River valley, the library wing was constructed in 1977 and the complex reached completion in 1987 with the construction of beautiful SWEENEY CHAPEL.

BUTLER UNIVERSITY, Sunset Avenue and 46th Street, is a coeducational private university that is now non-sectarian but was until 1958 affiliated with the Christian Church (Disciples of Christ). The institution began in 1855 as North West Christian University located at 13th Street and College Avenue on land donated by benefactor, Ovid Butler, for whom it was renamed in 1877. Historical Marker on College Avenue between 14th Street and the I-65 underpass designates its original site. Butler University moved to a twenty-five-acre campus in Irvington on the city's east side in 1875 before moving to the larger Sunset Avenue campus in 1928.

Sweeney Chapel, Christian Theological Seminary, Indianapolis, Marion County

The heart of campus includes a set of stately limestone collegiate Gothic Revival style buildings as well as buildings of contemporary design.

UNIVERSITY OF INDIANAPOLIS, 1400 East Hanna, is a coeducational liberal arts college affiliated with the United Methodist Church. Founded in 1905 as Indiana Central College by the United Brethren in Christ, which later was merged with the Evangelical Church to form the Evangelical United Brethren, which, in turn became part of the United Methodist Church. ★ GOOD HALL, the administration building, built in a Classical Revival style in 1905, once housed the entire college. NRHP

MARIAN COLLEGE, 3200 Cold Spring Road, is a coeducational Catholic liberal arts college founded by the Sisters of St. Francis of Oldenburg. The college developed from the Franciscan Sisters' normal school for their own members at Oldenburg, Indiana, which in 1937 was moved to Indianapolis and expanded to a four-year college for women. Men were admitted in 1954. Two outstanding campus buildings were the homes of Indianapolis industrialists, James A. Allison and Frank Wheeler. ★ The ALLISON MANSION is listed on the NRHP and HABS. The campus place of worship is the Bishop Joseph Chartrand Chapel located in Marian Hall.

AENON BIBLE COLLEGE, 3939 Meadows Drive, is the unaccredited school of ministry of the Pentecostal Assemblies of the World, the African American Oneness Pentecostal denomination.

INDIANA BIBLE COLLEGE, 3350 Carson Avenue, is the unaccredited school of ministry of the Oneness Pentecostal denomination, the United Pentecostal Church. College was moved to site from Seymour, Indiana, in 1988.

Downtown Indianapolis, within the city's original "Mile Square," bounded by North, East, South, and West streets, is the location of eight of the city's oldest congregations, six of which are listed on the NRHP:

🏛 ★ CHRIST CHURCH CATHEDRAL (Episcopal), Monument Circle, where several historic congregations were located in the city's early years. Now only Christ Church remains. The congregation dates from 1837; the stately English country Gothic style church designed by William J. Tinsley dates from 1857–1859. NRHP/HABS

🏛 ★ ROBERTS PARK UNITED METHODIST CHURCH, 401 N. Delaware Street, traces origins to city's first Methodist congregation founded in 1821. The city's leading nineteenth-century architect, Dietrich A. Bohlen, designed the present magnificent Romanesque Revival church building begun in 1876. NRHP

🏛 ★ ST. JOHN CATHOLIC CHURCH, S. Capitol Avenue and W. Georgia Street, the city's oldest Catholic parish was formed in 1837. D. A. Bohlen designed this imposing red brick Gothic Revival church constructed in 1867–1871. NRHP

★ ST. MARY'S CATHOLIC CHURCH, N. New Jersey and E. Vermont streets, the city's

Roberts Park United Methodist Church, Indianapolis, Marion County

Saint Mary's Catholic Church, Indianapolis, Marion County

second Catholic parish was founded for Germans in 1857 on E. Maryland Street. The present limestone Gothic structure imitating the Cologne Cathedral was built according to design of Herman Gaul in 1910–1912. NRHP

★ FIRST LUTHERAN CHURCH, 701 N. Pennsylvania Street, congregation formed in 1837 as Mt. Pisgah Lutheran Church. The Romanesque Revival church dates from 1875 with additions in 1886. NRHP

★ BETHEL AFRICAN METHODIST EPISCOPAL CHURCH, 414 W. Vermont Street, this red brick Romanesque Revival building dates from 1869 with later additions and modifications. Founded in 1836, Bethel is the city's oldest black congregation. NRHP

★ ZION EVANGELICAL UNITED CHURCH OF CHRIST, 601 N. New Jersey Street, founded in 1841 by German immigrants carrying on the tradition of German Evangelical state churches, red brick Gothic Revival building designed by D. A. Bohlen firm dates from 1912–1913.

Former SECOND BAPTIST CHURCH, W. Michigan and West streets, was home to the city's first African American Baptist congregation formed in 1846. Nineteenth-century pastor, Rev. Moses Broyles, was community leader and founder of an Indiana association of black Baptist churches. The Classic Revival building dates from 1884, rebuilt in 1912, and recently renovated for condominiums.

HISTORICAL MARKER, HOLY TRINITY GREEK ORTHODOX CHURCH, N. West Street near W. Ohio Street, on grounds of Fire Station No. 13, designates the site one block north of marker at 231 N. West Street, where Greek immigrants, who organized the city's first Orthodox congregation in 1910, maintained their church from 1919 to 1959. Holy Trinity Greek Orthodox Church is now located at 4011 N. Pennsylvania Street in buildings of modern design.

OTHER SITES IN CENTER TOWNSHIP:

🏛 ★ GOTHIC CHAPEL, CROWN HILL CEMETERY, 34th Street and Boulevard Place, is a splendid limestone church designed by D. A. Bohlen, built in 1875–1877, located in the city's historic cemetery. HABS. Crown Hill Cemetery is listed on NRHP.

★ STS. PETER AND PAUL CATHOLIC CATHEDRAL, N. Meridian and 14th streets, founded as a parish in 1892, the present Neo-Classical building was constructed in 1906–1907 according to design of New York architect William Renwick. The facade was designed by D. A. Bohlen firm and completed in 1936.

★ ACADEMY APARTMENTS, N. Meridian and 14th streets, opposite the above, was formerly St. Agnes Academy, a Catholic girls high school sponsored by Sisters of Providence; Italian Renaissance building designed by Bohlen firm was built about 1915.

★ CENTRAL CHRISTIAN CHURCH, 701 N. Delaware Street, red brick Romanesque

Revival complex dates from 1892, Peter P. Cookingham architect; the congregation, founded in 1833, is the city's first congregation of the Christian Church (Disciples of Christ).

★ Former ST. BRIDGET CATHOLIC CHURCH, 801 Dr. Martin Luther King Jr. Street, red brick Romanesque Revival church was built for Irish parishioners in 1879, later served black Catholics and campus ministry for nearby Indiana University-Purdue University at Indianapolis (IUPUI). Parish closed in 1994.

★ CENTRAL AVENUE UNITED METHODIST CHURCH, Central Avenue and E. 12th Street, a magnificent red brick Romanesque Revival monument built in 1891 in a fashionable neighborhood, congregation founded closer to downtown in 1854.

★ TABERNACLE PRESBYTERIAN CHURCH, 418 E. 34th Street, limestone Gothic structure dates from 1921, R. F. Daggett, architect. Congregation was organized in 1883 with antecedents as Third Presbyterian Church founded in 1851.

★ BROADWAY UNITED METHODIST CHURCH, Fall Creek Parkway and E. 29th Street, splendid limestone Gothic complex begun in 1925, founded at 16th Street site in 1873.

★ ASSEMBLY HALL OF JEHOVAH'S WITNESSES, 1201 N. Delaware Street, occupies the former Second Church of Christ, Scientist; this massive Neo-Classical building dating from 1912 was designed by Solon S. Beman.

CHRIST TEMPLE APOSTOLIC FAITH, 430 W. Fall Creek Parkway, was founded in 1918 under leadership of Bishop Garfield T. Haywood, Oneness Pentecostal founder. His denomination, Pentecostal Assemblies of the World, is one of the largest African American denominations in the United States. Its headquarters has been in Indianapolis since 1919.

★ PHILLIPS TEMPLE CHRISTIAN METHODIST EPISCOPAL CHURCH, 210 E. 34th Street, built for Third Church of Christ, Scientist, in limestone Art Deco style in 1928, R. F. Daggett, architect. Phillips Temple, the city's historic CME congregation, moved to buildings in 1993, leaving its historic building on Dr. Martin Luther King Jr. Street, next to Crispus Attucks High School.

★ LOCKERBIE SQUARE UNITED METHODIST CHURCH, New York and East streets, formerly Evangelical United Brethren Church, D. A. Bohlen firm designed this red brick Romanesque Revival church built in 1892. Congregation formed by Evangelical Association in 1855.

★ HOLY CROSS CATHOLIC CHURCH, E. Ohio and Oriental streets, buff brick with limestone facade, this Italian Renaissance Revival building was designed by Cornelius Curtin and built in 1921, parish was founded in 1895.

★ WOODRUFF PLACE BAPTIST CHURCH, E. Michigan and Walcott streets, congrega-

Central Christian Church, Indianapolis, Marion County

Christ Temple, Indianapolis, Marion County

tion formed in 1904, a fine brick Italian Renaissance Revival church built in 1926, located at the city's early residential suburb, Woodruff Place.

★ MARTIN UNIVERSITY PERFORMING ARTS CENTER, 2195 N. Avondale Place, occupies the former St. Francis de Sales Catholic Church, a red brick Bavarian Baroque style structure built in 1913 according to design of George Bedell.

JONES TABERNACLE AME ZION CHURCH, 2510 E. 34th Street, historic African Methodist Episcopal Zion Church in city founded in 1872–1873, occupies a set of buildings of contemporary design.

★ KOALA HOSPITAL, 1404 S. State Avenue, occupies building of the former General German Protestant Orphan Home later called Pleasant Run Children's Home. The Victorian Gothic building designed by D. A. Bohlen was built in 1871. The orphanage was founded by city's German Evangelical churches to care for German Protestant orphans. NRHP

★ ST. PATRICK CATHOLIC CHURCH, 951 Woodlawn Street, a brick and limestone Spanish Renaissance Revival structure designed by Adolf Scherrer and dates from 1928 for parish that Irish immigrants formed in 1865.

★ IMMANUEL UNITED CHURCH OF CHRIST, 402 E. Prospect Street, formerly Immanuel Evangelical and Reformed Church, a fine Romanesque Revival building dating from 1894, congregation formed in 1880.

★ SACRED HEART CATHOLIC CHURCH, 1530 S. Union Street, red brick Gothic Revival building dates from 1883–1891, parish founded as city's second German Catholic congregation in 1875.

★ Former FLETCHER PLACE UNITED METHODIST CHURCH, Fletcher Avenue at South and East streets. A congregation with close ties to early city father Calvin Fletcher, the imposing red brick Gothic Revival church dates from 1872.

★ HOLY ROSARY CATHOLIC CHURCH, Stevens and East streets, parish founded for the city's Italian Catholics in 1909, red brick Classical Revival building designed by J. Edwin Kopf and Kenneth Wooling dates from 1925.

★ CHURCH OF JESUS CHRIST APOSTOLIC FAITH, E. McCarty and Noble streets, a small red brick Gothic Revival church built in 1872 for Trinity Evangelical Lutheran Church, the first Danish ethnic congregation formed in the United States.

ST. JOSEPH CHAPEL, ST. JOSEPH-HOLY CROSS CEMETERY, S. Meridian Street and Pleasant Run Parkway, S. Drive, a pleasing, small red brick Gothic Revival structure built in 1874, located on a rise in the city's historic Catholic cemetery.

CALVARY TABERNACLE, 902 Fletcher Avenue, sanctuary seats 2,800 in one of the country's major congregations of the United Pentecostal Church. Rev. Nathaniel

Urshan, pastor in the 1950s, was a national leader among United Pentecostals. Denomination's Indiana Bible College, 3350 Carson Avenue, with close ties to Calvary Tabernacle, was moved from Seymour, Indiana in 1988.

ALLEN CHAPEL AFRICAN METHODIST EPISCOPAL CHURCH, 11th Street and Broadway, an imposing red brick Classical Revival structure, built in 1927–1929 for congregation formed in 1866.

HISTORICAL MARKER, ST. STEPHEN BULGARIAN ORTHODOX CHURCH, Blackford and New York streets, east side of IUPUI Law School, marks original site of church from 1915 to 1955. Founded by Macedonian and Bulgarian immigrants, the church is now located at 1435 N. Medford Avenue.

WASHINGTON TOWNSHIP:

SECOND PRESBYTERIAN CHURCH, 7700 N. Meridian Street, a magnificent structure in French Gothic style influenced by Sainte Chapelle in Paris, built in 1958, McGuire, Shook, Compton, and Richey architects. Congregation was organized in 1838. Early minister Henry Ward Beecher later gained national prominence as leading Protestant clergyman.

NORTH UNITED METHODIST CHURCH, N. Meridian and 38th streets, is a splendid structure built in 1925–1931 according to plans of Neo-Gothic architect, Charles H. Hopson, for this fashionable northside congregation. The congregation had been formed in 1843 closer to downtown area.

FIRST-MERIDIAN HEIGHTS PRESBYTERIAN CHURCH, 4701 N. Central Avenue, is an excellent limestone Gothic building dating from 1927. The congregation resulted from merger of Meridian Heights Presbyterian Church, founded at the site in 1909, with First Presbyterian Church, founded in 1823 and located at 16th and Delaware streets, where President Benjamin Harrison was elder.

MERIDIAN STREET UNITED METHODIST CHURCH, 5500 N. Meridian Street, was built in a magnificent Colonial Revival style in 1949–1952 according to design of Merritt Harrison. Church traces origins to the city's first Methodist congregation founded in 1821.

ST. JOAN OF ARC CATHOLIC CHURCH, N. Central Avenue and E. 42nd Street, is a massive Italian Renaissance structure with soaring campanile built in 1928–1929 of Indiana limestone. Noted Chicago architect Henry Schlacks designed structure for parish formed in 1921.

BETHLEHEM LUTHERAN CHURCH, N. Central Avenue and E. 52nd Street, founded in 1923; the limestone Neo-Gothic style church was built in 1929–1930. Former pastor Donald E. Elder was noted for encouraging an interest in religious art as reflected in the splendid triptych behind the altar.

INDIANAPOLIS HEBREW CONGREGATION, 6501 N. Meridian Street, is the city's congregation representing Reform Judaism. The temple of a striking modern design was built in 1956–1958. Founded in 1856 as the city's first Jewish congregation, its temple was located at Delaware and 10th streets from 1899 to 1958.

CONGREGATION BETH-EL ZEDECK, 600 W. 70th Street, is a congregation associated with Conservative and Reconstructionist Judaism. The building of contemporary functional design dates from 1957–1958. The congregation had earlier met at a temple located at Ruckle and 34th streets. Beth-El Zedeck resulted from mergers of Sharah Tefilla (Polish), Ohev Zedeck (Hungarian), and Knesses Israel (Russian) congregations.

CONGREGATION B'NAI TORAH, 65th Street and Hoover Road, is the city's largest congregation representing Orthodox Judaism. Formed in 1957 as the result of the merger of two older congregations, it moved in 1967 to building of contemporary design.

WARREN TOWNSHIP:

★ ST. JOHN'S EVANGELICAL LUTHERAN CHURCH, 6750 Southeastern Avenue, red brick Tudor Revival/Jacobethan structure built in 1927, parish formed in 1852.

ST. JOHN UNITED CHURCH OF CHRIST, E. Washington Street and German Church Road, Warren Township, formed as German Evangelical congregation in 1855, dark brick twentieth-century Gothic Revival church was built in 1913.

The eastside Irvington neighborhood, dating from the 1870s, is the historic Indianapolis suburb noted for many fine residences. The local residents sustained congregations with these excellent church buildings:

★ IRVINGTON UNITED METHODIST CHURCH, 30 N. Audubon Road, near E. Washington Street, formed in 1877, the present church, built in 1926 in an exceptionally beautiful English Gothic style, is encircled by Audubon Place with its fine residences. Both the church building and its setting make this site a place of rare beauty in the city.

★ IRVINGTON PRESBYTERIAN CHURCH, Julian and Johnson avenues, is an impressive limestone Neo-Gothic church begun in 1928 for a congregation founded in 1906.

★ OUR LADY OF LOURDES CATHOLIC CHURCH, E. Washington Street at Downey Avenue, parish was formed in 1909. The present Indiana sandstone Gothic church was completed in 1942.

FOURTH CHURCH OF CHRIST, SCIENTIST, 5201 E. Pleasant Run Parkway S. Drive, is a limestone building with a Neo-Georgian appearance begun in 1936 for congregation formed in 1922. The setting on the wooded parkway enhances its beauty.

Indianapolis Hebrew Congregation, Indianapolis, Marion County

WAYNE TOWNSHIP:

★ ST. ANTHONY CATHOLIC CHURCH, N. Warman Avenue and W. Vermont Street, founded in 1891 for Catholics in Haughville, later annexed to Indianapolis, the present Victorian Gothic building designed by Cornelius Curtin was constructed in 1904.

★ HOLY TRINITY CATHOLIC CHURCH, N. Holmes Avenue and W. St. Clair Street, was founded in 1906 for the Slovenian immigrants living in Haughville. The present dark brick Romanesque Revival church was built in 1906–1907 according to design of George Bedell.

★ GIRLS SCHOOL CHAPEL, 2596 Girls School Road, a stately brick Georgian Revival building constructed in 1938 on campus of state school.

LAKEVIEW CHRISTIAN CENTER, 47 Beachway Drive at Rockville Road Exit on I-465, affiliated with the Assemblies of God, was founded in 1912 by Maria Beulah Woodworth-Etter, one of the first women Pentecostal evangelists of national influence. First location was on Miller Street before moving to present building where many of the congregation's social services and activities are located.

MONASTERY OF THE RESURRECTION, DISCALCED CARMELITES, 2500 Cold Spring Road, convent of historic Catholic women's contemplative order; nuns reside in unique building designed by J. Edwin Kopf with Old World monastic appearance, dates from 1932.

PERRY TOWNSHIP:

★ HOLY NAME CATHOLIC CHURCH, 89 N. 17th Avenue, Beech Grove, brick and limestone Art Deco style church built in 1953, parish formed in 1908.

LAWRENCE TOWNSHIP:

UNITARIAN-UNIVERSALIST CHURCH, N. Oaklandon Boulevard and E. 64th Street, Oaklandon, brick gable-front church erected in 1875 and rebuilt in 1921. The congregation was organized in 1838 and was one of the state's last active Universalist congregations before merger with Unitarians in 1961.

★ Former OAKLANDON CHRISTIAN CHURCH, N. Oaklandon Boulevard and E. 64th Street, Oaklandon, elegant frame Gothic Revival structure built in 1909, used by other congregations and as a private residence.

PIKE TOWNSHIP:

★ SALEM LUTHERAN CHURCH, 72nd and Pollard streets, New Augusta, Pike Township, congregation organized in 1836 as Hopewell Lutheran Church, one of oldest in the county, red brick Romanesque Revival church dates from 1880.

★ BETHEL UNITED METHODIST CHURCH, 5252 W. 52nd Street, east of Lafayette Road, red brick Gothic Revival church built in 1905 for congregation formed in 1832. Large historic cemetery is nearby.

★ HISTORICAL MARKER, MOUNT PLEASANT MISSIONARY BAPTIST CHURCH, Reed Road between 56th and 62nd streets in Eagle Creek Park, commemorates the African-American house of worship that was founded in Pike Township in 1893 and stood at site from 1930 to 1972. Congregation now worships at 5111 W. 62nd Street.

FRANKLIN TOWNSHIP:

FRANKLIN TOWNSHIP HISTORICAL SOCIETY, 6510 S. Franklin Road at Indian Creek Road, former Big Run Baptist Church, a red brick Italianate structure built in 1871, congregation founded in 1848.

MORGAN COUNTY

Morgan County with its rural and small-town traditions has increasingly become a part of greater Indianapolis. The county's leading religious groups are Christian Church or Church of Christ, Southern Baptists, and American Baptists. Martinsville, Washington Township, the county seat, boasts the following historic churches:

★ FIRST PRESBYTERIAN CHURCH, E. Washington and Sycamore streets, founded as a Cumberland Presbyterian congregation in 1841, red brick Gothic Revival church in excellent condition dates from 1880–1881.

★ PRINCE OF PEACE LUTHERAN CHURCH, E. Pike and N. Wayne streets, formerly the city's Catholic church, a small red brick Gothic Revival gem built in 1888.

FIRST CHRISTIAN CHURCH, S. Main and Jackson streets, a fine red brick Gothic Revival structure dating from 1891, congregation organized in 1835.

ELSEWHERE IN MORGAN COUNTY:

★ WAVERLY UNITED METHODIST CHURCH, Main Street, Waverly, Harrison Township, Queen Anne style building dates from 1890, noted for fine craftsmanship and detail in wood structure. Congregation dates from 1850s.

MOORESVILLE UNITED METHODIST CHURCH, S. Indiana and E. Harrison streets, Mooresville, Brown Township, congregation organized in 1833, red brick Gothic Revival structure erected in 1882.

MOORESVILLE FRIENDS ACADEMY BUILDING, 234 N. Monroe, Mooresville, Brown Township, red brick Victorian building, nearby at Monroe and W. Main is the White Lick Meeting of Friends, established in 1823, housed in a red brick building with several additions. Academy is listed on NRHP.

FIRST CHRISTIAN CHURCH, Washington near Highland Street, Morgantown, Jackson Township, simple gable-front red brick building, built in 1871, congregation dates from 1840s.

SHELBY COUNTY

Shelby County has a long history of industry and agriculture as well as the influence of such leading religious bodies as American Baptists, United Methodists, and Catholics. Shelbyville, Addison Township, the county seat, is the site of several of the county's most impressive churches:

★ FIRST PRESBYTERIAN CHURCH, W. Broadway and Tomkins streets, congregation organized in 1824, present red brick Gothic Revival church built in 1885.

★ FIRST CHRISTIAN CHURCH, W. Washington and N. Tomkins streets, erected in 1901 in limestone Gothic Revival style with later additions, congregation started in 1834.

★ FIRST BAPTIST CHURCH, W. Washington and Tomkins streets, red brick Gothic Revival style house of worship erected in 1876 and rebuilt in 1902, congregation organized in 1826.

★ ST. JOSEPH CATHOLIC CHURCH, E. Broad Street near Noble Street, is an imposing Renaissance Revival church designed by Cornelius Curtin and built in 1903–1908, parish was formed in 1868.

OTHER SITES IN SHELBY COUNTY:

HISTORICAL MARKER, SITE OF BRANDYWINE CHURCH where Regular Baptist Convention of Indiana was formed in 1833, Michigan Road and CR 325W, near Fairland, Brandywine Township; location is 1.7 miles north of Exit 109 on I-74. Before Interstate highway was built, the marker was located 2950 feet north and 27.5 degrees east of present location.

★ ST. GEORGE LUTHERAN CHURCH, SR 252 and CR 600W, Jackson Township, this fine red brick Romanesque Revival church was built in 1867, congregation formed in 1838. NRHP

★ ST. VINCENT DE PAUL CATHOLIC CHURCH, Michigan Road near I-74 Exit 119, Liberty Township, is a brick Gothic Revival church erected in 1924. Parish was established in 1837, when its resident priest, Vincent Bacquelin, also ministered to the Catholics of Indianapolis.

★ WALDRON UNITED METHODIST CHURCH, Pullam and Main streets, Waldron, Liberty Township, this imposing twentieth-century Gothic Revival structure dates from 1924 and was damaged by explosion in 1995, congregation formed in 1836.

★ ZION UNITED CHURCH OF CHRIST, CR 700E and 100N, Union Township, twentieth-century Gothic Revival church built in 1929–1930, organized as German Evangelical congregation by immigrants in 1836.

★ FAIRLAND UNITED METHODIST CHURCH, Washington and Mulberry streets, Fairland, Brandywine Township, founded as Grace Methodist Episcopal Church in 1855, present elegant red brick Romanesque Revival structure built in 1893.

MT. AUBURN CHRISTIAN CHURCH, CR 900S, Jackson Township, red brick Romanesque Revival church built in 1903 surrounded by cemetery, congregation dates from 1837.

ST. PAUL UNITED METHODIST CHURCH, N. Jackson and Franklin streets, St. Paul, Noble Township, an impressive red brick Gothic Revival structure built in 1892, congregation started in 1859.

ST. PAUL CHRISTIAN CHURCH, N. Webster and Harrison streets, St. Paul, Noble Township, twentieth-century Gothic Revival structure rebuilt in 1925 for congregation founded in 1874, church building was formerly "union" meeting house of several local congregations.

BETHEL SEPARATE BAPTIST CHURCH, Vandalia Rd and CR 727E, Noble Township, carpenter built church with bell visible in belfry, congregation founded in 1847.

TIPTON COUNTY

Tipton County with its characteristic flatness is an ideal farming area. Leading religious bodies in the county include Christian Church (Disciples of Christ), Catholic, and United Methodist. The county seat, Tipton, Cicero Township, is the location of the following historic churches:

KEMP UNITED METHODIST CHURCH, N. Main and Walnut streets, Gothic Revival church built in 1903–1904, named in memory of wife of principal donor, Abraham Kemp, congregation organized in 1845.

ST. JOHN THE BAPTIST CATHOLIC CHURCH, E. North and N. Mill streets, large Gothic Revival church built in 1891 for parish formed in 1874.

WEST STREET CHRISTIAN CHURCH, West and Washington streets, Romanesque Revival church built in 1905–1906, congregation organized in 1855.

FIRST UNITED PRESBYTERIAN CHURCH, West and Jefferson streets, twentieth-century Gothic Revival building dates from 1928, congregation organized in 1854.

OLD ST. JOHN'S LUTHERAN CHURCH, SR 19, southside of Tipton, on grounds of Emanuel Lutheran Church, was organized by German immigrants in the southeastern part of the county in 1859. The log structure was used as a house of worship until 1901 when Emanuel Lutheran in Tipton was founded. Log church was relocated to the grounds of Emanuel Lutheran Church in 1993 and is being restored.

ELSEWHERE IN TIPTON COUNTY:

NORMANDA CHRISTIAN CHURCH, Division Road and CR 800W, Normanda, Jefferson Township, is a fine Gothic Revival church built in 1906.

SISTERS OF ST. JOSEPH MOTHERHOUSE, Division Road (CR 00), a half mile west of SR 19, north of Tipton, Cicero Township. The founding Sisters of St. Joseph, a Catholic women's religious order, established the convent in 1888; their older buildings have all been removed. The Administration Center or motherhouse dating from 1957 is also used as a conference center.

East Central Region

BLACKFORD COUNTY

Blackford, one of the state's smaller counties, is home to farming and light industries. Today's leading religious groups are United Methodist, Church of the Nazarene, and Catholic. The county's major historic churches are concentrated in its two population centers, the county seat, Hartford City, and Montpelier.

FIRST PRESBYTERIAN CHURCH, N. High and W. Franklin streets, Hartford City, Licking Township, an excellent Romanesque Revival edifice dating from 1892–1893 for congregation organized in 1843. NRHP

ST. JOHN THE EVANGELIST CATHOLIC CHURCH, E. Water and S. Spring streets, Hartford City, Licking Township, perma stone Gothic Revival church built in 1897, parish formed in 1883.

GRACE UNITED METHODIST CHURCH, W. Washington and Cherry streets, Hartford City, Licking Township, an elegant twentieth-century Gothic revival building constructed in 1926 for the city's historic Methodist congregation formed in 1843.

TRINITY UNITED METHODIST CHURCH, N. Walnut and W. Franklin streets, Hartford City, Licking Township, a fine Neo-Classical building dating from 1926, constructed for the United Brethren congregation founded in 1882.

FIRST CHRISTIAN CHURCH, N. High and W. Franklin streets, Hartford City, Licking Township, painted brick Gothic Revival structure built in 1894 for congregation founded in 1889.

MONTPELIER CHURCH OF CHRIST, W. Huntington and Jefferson streets, Montpelier, Harrison Township, red brick twentieth-century Classical Revival structure built in 1921, congregation started in 1870.

FIRST UNITED METHODIST CHURCH, S. Adams and E. Green streets, Montpelier, Harrison Township, red brick Gothic Revival edifice built in 1895 and rebuilt in 1923, congregation formed in 1837.

FIRST BAPTIST CHURCH, E. Huntington and Main streets, Montpelier, Harrison Township, in 1881 a reorganized congregation built this red brick Gothic Revival church, rebuilt 1907.

DELAWARE COUNTY

The religious groups claiming allegiance of the largest number of Delaware County residents are the United Methodist Church, the Catholic Church, and independent charismatic congregations. Muncie, Center Township, the county seat and home of Ball State University, has gained fame as the quintessential average American city since Robert and Helen Lynd's influential sociological study, *Middletown: A Study in American Culture*, published in 1929. Follow-up studies have reexplored the same themes in the 1980s. Muncie's splendid collection of churches reveal the worship practices of an American "Middletown." The following historic congregations are located in the downtown neighborhood:

★ FIRST BAPTIST CHURCH, E. Adams and S. Jefferson streets, a truly magnificent limestone Gothic building begun in 1927 for a historic congregation formed in 1859. NRHP

★ HIGH STREET UNITED METHODIST CHURCH, S. High and W. Adams streets, is a splendid Gothic Revival building dating from 1929, congregation dates from 1836, the city's oldest.

★ MAIN STREET UNITED METHODIST CHURCH, E. Main and S. Pershing streets, a graceful Neo-Classical building dating from 1912, congregation formed in 1872.

★ MADISON STREET UNITED METHODIST CHURCH, S. Madison and E. 7th streets, dark brick Jacobean Revival building dating from 1925 for congregation organized in 1895.

★ ST. LAWRENCE CATHOLIC CHURCH, E. Charles and S. Hackley streets, red brick Gothic Revival edifice built in 1893, for parish started in 1869.

★ TEMPLE BETH-EL, W. Jackson and Council streets, a compact Classical Revival building dating from 1922 for the city's Jewish community.

★ FRIENDS MEMORIAL CHURCH, W. Adams and Cherry streets, a fine Gothic Revival complex dating from 1906–1907 for a congregation founded in 1876.

★ FIRST CHURCH OF CHRIST, SCIENTIST, 300 W. Charles Street, a fine stone Renaissance Revival building dating from 1929.

★ Former FIRST CHRISTIAN CHURCH, E. North and N. Elm streets, a red brick Romanesque Revival church built in 1902 for congregation organized in 1892; the church was been home to other congregations and organizations in recent years.

WESLEY CHAPEL CHURCH, W. Jackson and S. Council streets, red brick gable-front Gothic Revival church built for First Presbyterian Church in 1898.

OTHER SITES IN DELAWARE COUNTY:

★ MT. ZION UNITED METHODIST CHURCH, CR 1100N at 100W, Union Township, is a lovely red brick Greek Revival church built in 1867, surrounded by historic cemetery dating from 1840.

★ FIRST UNITED METHODIST CHURCH, Elm and South streets, Eaton, Union Township, Jacobethan Revival structure built in 1878, remodeled in 1902, rebuilt in 1924 after a fire, congregation founded in 1873.

★ GASTON UNITED METHODIST CHURCH, N. Main and Walnut streets, Gaston, Washington Township, Romanesque Revival church dating from 1894, rebuilt after fire of 1903, congregation was started in 1843.

★ CROSSROADS LUTHERAN CHURCH, CR 600W and 700S, Salem Township, founded as Richwood English Lutheran Church, a well maintained red brick Gothic Revival church was built in 1868, reorganized in 1866 from earlier efforts dating from 1843.

FAYETTE COUNTY

Fayette County, named for the Marquis of Lafayette, relies on agriculture as its main industry and is home of Shrader-Weaver Nature Preserve. The county's leading religious groups are Catholic, United Methodist, and independent congregations. The picturesque county seat, Connersville, is home to a group of historic churches:

★ ST. GABRIEL CATHOLIC CHURCH, 9th Street and Western Avenue, red brick Gothic Revival structure built in 1883 according to design of D. A. Bohlen, congregation was formed in 1851.

★ FIRST UNITED METHODIST CHURCH, Eighth and Central streets, massive limestone Gothic Revival structure dates from 1889, congregation started in 1822.

★ FIRST PRESBYTERIAN CHURCH, Seventh and Central streets, red brick Romanesque Revival church dating from 1870s for congregation organized in 1824.

★ CENTRAL CHRISTIAN CHURCH, Eighth and Central streets, opposite First Presbyterian, limestone Gothic Revival monument built in 1904, congregation formed in 1833.

TRINITY EPISCOPAL CHURCH, Eastern Avenue and E. Sixth Street, a modest red brick Gothic Revival building dating from 1853, congregation was formed in 1850.

OTHER SITES IN FAYETTE COUNTY:

★ VILLAGE CREEK PRIMITIVE BAPTIST CHURCH, CR 150E between Village Creek and

Alquina roads, Connersville Township, a wood gable-front Gothic Revival structure, built ca. 1860, historic cemetery surrounds church.

★ SPRINGERSVILLE CHRISTIAN CHURCH, CR 150N near 450E, Springersville, Waterloo Township, Eastlake style building erected in 1883, extensively remodeled in 1913.

★ ST. PAUL LUTHERAN CHURCH, CR 450E, near Lyonsville, Jennings Township, carpenter-built Romanesque Revival building dates from 1891, congregation formed in 1843.

★ ALQUINA UNITED METHODIST CHURCH, CR 450E and 200S, Alquina, Jennings Township, red brick Gothic Revival structure built in 1923, congregation established in 1819.

★ ORANGE CHRISTIAN CHURCH, CR 850W and 400S (North Street), Orange, Orange Township, Greek Revival building constructed in 1851 and rebuilt in 1875, congregation established in 1829.

★ ALPINE CHRISTIAN CHURCH, SR 121 and Patterson Road, Alpine, Columbia Township, simple frame gable-front structure built for Baptist congregation in 1850s, Christian congregation organized in 1898.

GRANT COUNTY

Grant County is noted for a balance of industry and agriculture and as the longtime home of two church-affiliated institutions of higher learning. The county's leading religious bodies are the Wesleyan Church, the United Methodist Church, and the Catholic Church. The county's major historic site located in Marion, Center Township, the county seat, is the George Jr. and Marie Daugherty Webster House. (NHL/NRHP) Marion is also home to these varied religious sites:

INDIANA WESLEYAN UNIVERSITY, S. Washington Street between 42nd and 43rd streets, known as Marion College until 1988, is a coeducational liberal arts college affiliated with the Wesleyan Church. The church purchased the former Marion Normal Institute in 1919 and chartered it the following year as Marion College, joining to it the church's Bible school previously located at Fairmount. The third floor of the Administration Building in the "Old Triangle" section of campus houses a small museum. Besides its denominational college, the Wesleyan Church's international headquarters was located in Marion until moving to Indianapolis in 1987.

WORLD GOSPEL MISSION HEADQUARTERS, SR 18 near CR 400E, east of Marion, is a building of modern design that is home to a Holiness missionary society founded in 1910. In the Wesleyan tradition, World Gospel Mission promotes interdenominational missions and missionary work in domestic and foreign fields and scriptural holiness through a properly qualified ministry.

Village Creek Primitive Baptist Church, Connersville Township, Fayette County

★ CHAPEL, NATIONAL MILITARY HOME, McMahon Avenue and Carey Road, an elegant red brick Gothic Revival structure built in 1899 for this old soldiers home.

★ FIRST PRESBYTERIAN CHURCH, W. Sixth and Gallatin streets, limestone twentieth-century Gothic Revival building resembling a medieval fortress dates from 1903–1904, congregation organized in 1843.

★ TRINITY VICTORY BAPTIST CHURCH, W. Fourth and Nebraska streets, former First Baptist Church, Marion's historic Baptist congregation formed in 1885, Classical Revival building dates from 1913.

★ TEMPLE OF FAITH, S. Adams and Fifteenth streets, formerly First Friends Church, an imposing buff brick twentieth-century Gothic Revival complex built in 1914; Marion's Friends congregation dates from 1832, founding year of monthly meeting.

★ ALLEN TEMPLE AFRICAN METHODIST EPISCOPAL CHURCH, S. Washington and E. 35th streets, an imposing red brick Romanesque Revival church built in 1901, congregation formed in 1873.

FIRST UNITED METHODIST CHURCH, S. Adams and 7th streets, an imposing set of twentieth-century Gothic Revival buildings dating from 1922–1923, congregation organized in 1832.

ELSEWHERE IN GRANT COUNTY:

TAYLOR UNIVERSITY, SR 22, Upland, Jefferson Township, is an independent Methodist coeducational liberal arts college. Founded in 1846 at Fort Wayne as the Fort Wayne Female College, the school was moved to Upland in 1893, renamed in honor of Methodist missionary, Bishop William Taylor, and admitted men. The campus is noteworthy for many attractive buildings of modern design including its place of worship, Rediger Chapel.

MIAMI INDIAN CEMETERY, CR 600N 1.1 miles west of SR 15, Pleasant Township. An Indian Baptist Church and school were located here, part of the last Indian reservation in Indiana. In the cemetery, few graves are marked. Burial was contrary to Indian religious practices and reflects Christian influence.

★ HOLY FAMILY CATHOLIC CHURCH, E. North A and N. 4th streets, Gas City, Mill Township, a stately red brick Gothic Revival church built in 1908 for congregation dating from 1893.

Fairmount, Fairmount Township, is famed as the hometown of James Dean, the young actor whose tragic death in 1955 created a personality cult. Thousands of his fans annually visit this classic small town to honor him, which is home to these notable churches:

★ FAIRMOUNT WESLEYAN CHURCH, Walnut and Third streets, a very attractive brick twentieth-century Gothic Revival church built around 1910, congregation organized in 1865.

★ FAIRMOUNT FIRST UNITED METHODIST CHURCH, Walnut and Jefferson streets, excellent red brick Gothic Revival church built in 1909, congregation founded by the 1850s.

FAIRMOUNT FRIENDS MEETING, W. First and Mill streets, red brick Romanesque Revival building dates from 1891–1892, a reminder of Quaker origins of the area, congregation started in 1871.

HENRY COUNTY

Henry County, the "Raintree County" of Hoosier author Ross Lockridge's famed novel of Quaker life, is also noted as the birthplace of aviation pioneers, Orville and Wilbur Wright. Though Quaker influence was once strong, other Christian bodies have become influential such as United Methodists, Church of the Nazarene, and Christian Church (Disciples of Christ). Summit Lake State Park attracts visitors to the area. New Castle, Henry Township, the county seat and location of the Indiana High School Basketball Hall of Fame, is home to these historic congregations:

FIRST UNITED METHODIST CHURCH, Church and S. 14th streets, twentieth-century limestone Gothic Revival edifice erected in 1903, is New Castle's historic Methodist congregation dating from 1827.

★ ST. ANNE CATHOLIC CHURCH, E. Broad and 19th streets, an imposing brick Romanesque Revival church built in 1923, parish dates from 1873.

FOURSQUARE GOSPEL CHURCH, 3200 S. 14th Street, is one of the state's largest congregations of the International Church of the Foursquare Gospel, a denomination associated with famed evangelist, Aimee Semple McPherson.

Knightstown, Wayne Township, located on U.S. 40, the historic National Road, is a picturesque town with many historic buildings including the following churches:

★ BETHEL PRESBYTERIAN CHURCH, S. Franklin and Jackson streets, a magnificent example of twentieth-century Classical Revival style in brick and limestone, dating from 1912. Congregation organized in 1832.

★ UNITED METHODIST CHURCH, S. Jefferson and Jackson streets, red brick Gothic Revival structure in pristine condition, dates from 1885, third building of a congregation formed in 1824.

OTHER SITES IN HENRY COUNTY:

SPICELAND FRIENDS MEETING, W. Main Street at Cemetery Drive, Italianate red brick church built in 1874. Marker notes former site of Spiceland Academy, which Friends formed in 1827 and became a leading secondary school. A famous graduate was Charles Beard, American historian.

HILLSBORO CHURCH OF CHRIST, CR 250N half mile east of Hillsboro Road, Hillsboro, Prairie Township, organized in 1839 and is said to be the oldest Church of Christ congregation in the state. Its stark lines recall the simplicity of early houses of worship. Site of scenes in Ross Lockridge's novel *Raintree County*.

★ LEWISVILLE PRESBYTERIAN CHURCH, U.S. 40 and 2nd Street, Lewisville, Franklin Township, gem-like red brick Gothic Revival structure dates from 1882, congregation formed in 1831.

★ NEW LIGHT CHRISTIAN CHURCH, N. Seventh and Columbia streets, Middletown, Fall Creek Township, handsome Romanesque Revival building dates from 1891.

UNITED METHODIST CHURCH, High Street between Sixth and Seventh streets, Middletown, Fall Creek Township, limestone fortress in twentieth-century Gothic Revival style built in 1901.

SIXTH STREET CHRISTIAN CHURCH, Sixth Street north of Locust Street, Middletown, Fall Creek Township, Disciples of Christ congregation formed by 1850, brick twentieth-century Gothic Revival building, dates from 1914.

SPRINGPORT CHRISTIAN CHURCH, Main and 3rd streets, Springport, Prairie Township, red brick twentieth-century Classical Revival structure, massive in appearance for a small-town place of worship. Congregation formed in 1879.

MOORELAND CHRISTIAN CHURCH, Broad Street, Mooreland, Blue Creek Township, excellent white frame Romanesque Revival church built in 1916, congregation formed in 1848.

★ BATSON CHRISTIAN CHURCH, CR 500E near SR 38, Liberty Township, Greek Revival-Italianate structure built around 1865, historic cemetery dates from 1823.

JAY COUNTY

Located on the Ohio border, Jay County is a typical Hoosier farming area. Today's largest religious groupings are United Methodist, Catholic, and the Church of the Nazarene. The county seat, Portland, Wayne Township, is location for some of the county's significant churches:

★ ASBURY UNITED METHODIST CHURCH, E. Arch and N. Harrison streets, fine stone Gothic Revival building dating from 1898–1903 for congregation organized in 1838.

★ CHURCH (UNNAMED), North Commerce and West Arch streets, is a well designed red brick Gothic Revival structure built in 1888.

★ FIRST PRESBYTERIAN CHURCH, W. Arch and N. Ship streets, a fine brick Gothic Revival church building dates from 1902, congregation formed in 1841.

★ FIRST UNITED BRETHREN CHURCH, S. Meridian and E. Third streets, a fine Classical Revival building constructed in 1916.

OTHER SITES IN JAY COUNTY:

★ HOLY TRINITY CATHOLIC CHURCH, SR 67, 6.1 miles east of U.S. 27, Wabash Township, Catholic parish founded among German immigrants in 1854, red brick Gothic Revival church dates from 1885. NRHP

★ UNITED METHODIST CHURCH, Main and Oak streets, Redkey, Richland Township, present splendid Romanesque Revival building dates from 1890 for congregation founded around 1845.

★ PLYMOUTH UNITED CHURCH OF CHRIST, S. Main and Pleasant streets, Dunkirk, Richland Township, Romanesque Revival structure built in 1896, founded as Congregational church in 1891.

HISTORICAL MARKER, WEST GROVE QUAKER SETTLEMENT, CR 30, east of CR 1 at West Grove Cemetery, designates site of early Quaker settlement, established in 1836, and became center of Underground Railroad activity for African Americans fleeing slavery.

MADISON COUNTY

Madison County is the location of one of the state's earliest Protestant missionary efforts, the Moravian Mission, established in 1801 when John Kluge and his wife arrived from Pennsylvania to minister to Delaware Indians on the White River east of what became Anderson. After many hardships and limited success, they departed in 1806. The county attracts visitors to Mounds State Park, location of earthworks constructed by prehistoric residents about 160 B.C. (NRHP) Today the county's religious bodies claiming the most adherents are Catholic, United Methodist, and the Church of God (Anderson).

The following sites are located in Anderson, the Madison County seat:

HISTORICAL MARKER, E. 10th and Moravian streets, .4 mile east of SR 9, a small limestone shaft erected by Daughters of the American Revolution commemorates the MORAVIAN MISSION described above. The mission's actual site is about two miles south of marker on the White River.

ANDERSON UNIVERSITY, College Drive between 3rd and 5th streets, is a coeducational liberal arts college and Theological Seminary affiliated with the Church of

God (Anderson). The school began as the Anderson College and Theological Seminary in 1925 with the Graduate School of Theology established in 1950. The attractive campus includes many buildings of modern design. The Museum of Bible and Near Eastern Studies at the School of Theology features exhibits related to the culture of Bible lands. The Jessie C. Wilson Galleries devote a room to the paintings of Warner Sallman whose famous "Head of Christ" is a favorite among Protestants and has been reproduced more than 500 million times.

CHURCH OF GOD (ANDERSON) EXECUTIVE OFFICES, 1303 E. Fifth Street, south side of Anderson University's campus, is the international office of the Church of God (Anderson). In an adjacent building is the denomination's Warner Press Publishers of the Church of God. Nearby on College Drive at Third Street is the imposing PARK PLACE CHURCH OF GOD, an attractive complex of contemporary design.

★ CENTRAL CHRISTIAN CHURCH, S. Jackson and Tenth streets, a triumphant limestone Spanish Baroque monument built in 1899–1900, congregation dates from 1858.

★ CENTRAL COMMUNITY CHAPEL, Tenth and Chase streets, founded as Hope Congregational Church, Romanesque Revival structure built in 1895 for congregation organized 1891.

★ ST. MARY CATHOLIC CHURCH, E. 11th and Fletcher streets, red brick Romanesque Revival building dates from 1893, parish founded in 1857.

ELSEWHERE IN MADISON COUNTY:

★ EAST CHRISTIAN CHURCH, E. Main Street (SR 38) at Sanders Drive, Markleville, Adams Township, small, fine red brick late Gothic Revival church built in 1914.

★ RIGDON UNITED METHODIST CHURCH, CR 600W and SR 37, Rigdon, Duck Creek Township, red brick Gothic Revival building begun in 1909, congregation formed in 1856.

★ HARMONY CHRISTIAN CHURCH, CR 1800N near SR 13, Leisure, Duck Creek Township, red brick Romanesque Revival building dates from 1913, congregation organized in 1885.

★ FIRST UNITED METHODIST CHURCH, N. A and Anderson streets, Elwood, Pipe Creek Township, beautiful limestone Gothic Revival church dating from 1899, founded in 1853.

★ ST. JOSEPH CATHOLIC CHURCH, S. A Street between S. Twelfth and Anderson streets, Elwood, Pipe Creek Township, an imposing red brick Romanesque Revival church with twin towers begun in 1899, parish founded in 1881.

★ FIRST UNITED METHODIST CHURCH, W. Broadway and Canal streets, Alexandria,

Park Place Church of God, Anderson University, Anderson, Madison County

Monroe Township, red brick Late Gothic Revival structure built in 1901, congregation started in 1836.

INDIANA ASSOCIATION OF SPIRITUALISTS CAMP, North Street, Chesterfield, Union Township, an institution of national importance to Spiritualists. The site began as a camp in the 1890s and has evolved into a residential village with accommodations for visitors. At the site is one of the world's largest schools for mediums. A museum features exhibits on Spiritualist manifestations and movements.

RANDOLPH COUNTY

Randolph County, with its agricultural economy, is also noted as the area of highest elevation in the state. The county's religious composition is mainly United Methodist, Christian Church (Disciples of Christ), Church of the Nazarene, and Friends (Quakers). The county seat, Winchester, White River Township, is home to the following historic churches:

WINCHESTER FRIENDS MEETING, 124 E. Washington Street, red brick Romanesque Revival building erected in 1897, its imposing size reflects the Friends' substantial presence in the county, though the town's Friends congregation was not started until 1873.

FIRST PRESBYTERIAN CHURCH, S. East and E. Franklin streets, limestone twentieth-century Gothic Revival structure built in 1902–1903, congregation organized in 1845.

FIRST UNITED METHODIST CHURCH, S. Meridian and Will streets, is a finely maintained red brick Gothic Revival church erected in 1900, congregation founded in 1822.

MAIN STREET CHRISTIAN CHURCH, Main and W. South streets, twentieth-century Classical Revival building erected in 1912–1914, congregation organized in 1866.

Union City, Wayne Township, an industrial community on the Ohio border, is Randolph County's other major population center with the following historic congregations:

WESLEY UNITED METHODIST CHURCH, W. Oak and N. Plum streets, a truly magnificent limestone monument in an elegant Gothic Revival style built in 1907, congregation established in 1852.

CHURCH OF CHRIST, N. Plum and W. Oak streets, occupying the corner opposite Wesley United Methodist, started in 1858. The present church was built in 1878, but successive remodelings in 1901 and after the 1914 fire have altered the character of this fine stucco Gothic Revival building.

ST. MARY CATHOLIC CHURCH, N. Plum and W. Hickory streets, a block away from the preceding two churches, is a red brick Gothic Revival structure built in 1891, parish formed in 1856.

UNITED PRESBYTERIAN CHURCH, N. Howard and W. Hickory streets, a fine modest white frame Queen Anne-Gothic Revival building dating from 1879, congregation founded in 1835 in nearby Ohio and relocated to Union City in 1862.

OTHER SITES IN RANDOLPH COUNTY:

BETHEL AFRICAN METHODIST EPISCOPAL CHURCH, SR 1 north of U.S. 36, Modoc, Union Township, a simple frame building still in use is a reminder of the founding generation of nineteenth-century Quakers who brought freed slaves to Indiana from North Carolina.

BETHEL UNITED METHODIST CHURCH, W. First and S. Race streets, Ridgeville, Franklin Township, excellent red brick Gothic Revival church dates from 1888, congregation started in 1856.

RUSH COUNTY

Rush County is noted as one of the finest agricultural areas in the state. Though Friends were prominent in the county's early years, today's leading religious bodies are Christian Church or Church of Christ, United Methodist, and Christian Church (Disciples of Christ). The county seat, Rushville, boasts a stately northside residential neighborhood, the location of the following outstanding churches:

★ FIRST PRESBYTERIAN CHURCH, N. Morgan and W. 3rd streets, a fine Romanesque Revival building dating from 1891. The congregation was organized in 1825. Wendell Willkie, 1940 Republican presidential nominee, was a member.

★ ST. PAUL'S UNITED METHODIST CHURCH, N. Morgan and W. 5th streets, an excellent red brick Victorian Gothic structure built in 1886, congregation dates from 1824.

★ MAIN STREET CHRISTIAN CHURCH, N. Main near W. 7th Street, a worthy Romanesque Revival church built in 1893, congregation organized in 1840.

★ ST. MARY CATHOLIC CHURCH, N. Perkins and E. 5th streets, an imposing red brick Romanesque Revival monument built in 1897 for parish founded in 1857.

★ TRINITY UNITED PRESBYTERIAN CHURCH, N. Harrison and W. 7th streets, a fine Gothic Revival structure built in 1915, congregation formed in 1879.

OTHER SITES IN RUSH COUNTY:

★ EBENEZER PRESBYTERIAN CHURCH, CR 1200N near 700E, Washington Township, a red brick Gothic Revival gem built in 1903, for congregation formed in 1831.

★ LINCOLN HALL (CHAPEL), Indiana Soldiers' and Sailors' Children's Home, SR 140, Knightstown, Center Township, a fine Romanesque Revival structure built in 1891.

🏛 ★ MT. PLEASANT BEECH AFRICAN METHODIST EPISCOPAL CHURCH, CR 725W, .3 mile north of 1000N, about 100 yards east of road, near Carthage, Ripley Township, the state's oldest African American congregation. Freed slaves who came to the area with Quakers from North Carolina formed "Old Beech" in 1832 and built this simple gable-front house of worship. The Indiana Conference of the African Methodist Episcopal Church was formed here in 1840.

★ WALNUT RIDGE FRIENDS MEETINGHOUSE, CR 800N and 900W, Ripley Township, red brick Federal style church built in 1866, founded in 1821 by Quakers from North Carolina who settled in the area. NRHP

★ Former MARKET STREET CHURCH OF CHRIST, N. Market Street near 3rd Street, Carthage, Ripley Township, gable-front structure built in 1875 (closed 1954), noteworthy as a congregation to which both whites and blacks belonged.

★ FLETCHER UNITED METHODIST CHURCH, N. East and E. 3rd streets, Carthage, Ripley Township, excellent Romanesque Revival building dating from 1897, congregation formed in 1857.

★ CARTHAGE FRIENDS MEETING, S. Main Street, Carthage, Ripley Township, gable-front structure was built in 1881, congregation formed in 1840. Friends Academy here began around 1870.

★ GLENWOOD UNITED METHODIST CHURCH, State Street (SR 44), Glenwood, Union Township, red brick Gothic Revival church built in 1920, congregation was organized in the 1840s.

★ CHRISTIAN UNION CHURCH, CR 725W, Homer, Walker Township, Gothic Revival building, congregation formed in 1868.

★ MANILLA CHRISTIAN CHURCH, Cross and Jackson streets, Manilla, Walker Township, Queen Anne style building dates from 1900, congregation organized in 1859.

★ CHRISTIAN CHURCH, Main and Gano streets, Milroy, Anderson Township, brick twentieth-century Neo-Classical structure built in 1916, congregation was founded in 1851.

★ UNITED PRESBYTERIAN CHURCH, S. Pleasant and W. South streets, Milroy, Anderson Township, Colonial Revival structure built in 1912, congregation dates from 1835.

★ MILROY UNITED METHODIST CHURCH, N. Pleasant and W. Church streets, Milroy,

Mount Pleasant Beech African Methodist Episcopal Church,
Ripley Township, Rush County

Walnut Ridge Friends Meetinghouse, Ripley Township, Ripley County

Anderson Township, Gothic Revival building dates from 1909, congregation established in 1837.

★ Former HOPEWELL UNITED BRETHREN CHURCH, CR 700E and 1000S, Richland Township, gable-front structure built in 1850, historic cemetery surrounds church.

UNION COUNTY

Union, the state's third smallest county in area, has a large history reflected in many fine old buildings. Among the county's attractions is the Whitewater Memorial State Park. Today's leading religious bodies include United Methodists, Catholics, and the Church of the Nazarene. Liberty, Center Township, the county seat, is noted as hometown of Civil War General Ambrose Burnside and the home of several exceptional churches:

FIRST PRESBYTERIAN CHURCH, N. Fairgrounds and E. Main streets, a red brick Romanesque Revival building in magnificent condition erected in 1889, congregation organized in 1829.

EDWARDS MEMORIAL UNITED METHODIST CHURCH, W. Seminary and S. Market streets, facing courthouse square, congregation dates from 1831, present splendid red brick Romanesque Revival church dates from 1885.

ST. BRIDGET CATHOLIC CHURCH, E. Vine and Flint streets, parish dates from 1854, red brick Gothic Revival church built in 1904.

OTHER SITES IN UNION COUNTY:

FOUR MILE CHURCH OF THE BRETHREN (German Baptist Brethren), 9 Mile Road and CR 350W, Harrison Township, congregation organized in 1809, the oldest in the county, present building erected 1857, with later additions.

SPRING GROVE PRIMITIVE BAPTIST CHURCH, 9 Mile Road and CR 100W, Harrison Township, founded in 1869, white frame gable-front building.

HANNA'S CREEK CHRISTIAN CHURCH, near CR 350N, west of Kitchel, Harrison Township, dates from 1831, Christian restoration leaders, Barton W. Stone, Daniel Wilson, and David Purviance preached here, present red brick Gothic Revival church built in 1906.

SALEM FRIENDS MEETING, Salem Road near CR 175S, Salem, Center Township, congregation organized in 1818, frame gable-front structure dates from 1900, historic cemetery opposite building.

WAYNE COUNTY

Wayne County's settlement is associated with the Society of Friends (Quakers), who arrived in the area from the Carolinas early in the nineteenth century. The first Friends meeting was started in Richmond, the county seat, in 1807. By 1850, the concentration of Orthodox Quakers in Richmond and vicinity was greater than in Philadelphia, the Friends' colonial capital. Today the county's leading religious groups are Catholics, United Methodists, and Southern Baptists. Note that the HLF survey of Wayne County does not include the City of Richmond. The important sites in Richmond's Friends' history include the following:

🏛 EARLHAM COLLEGE, 1000 W. National Road, a coeducational liberal arts college associated with the Society of Friends. Founded in 1847 as Friends Boarding School, the college was given present name in 1859 for Earlham Hall, estate of the Gurney family, prominent English Quakers. The campus place of worship is the Stout Meetinghouse. Also the Earlham School of Religion, which prepares candidates for ministry, has been located here since 1963. Bethany Theological Seminary of the Church of the Brethren relocated here in 1993. NT

🏛 JULIA MEEK GARR WAYNE COUNTY HISTORICAL MUSEUM, N. A Street between N. 11th and N. 12th streets, red brick structure built in 1865 as Hicksite Friends Meetinghouse, and was home of this congregation of Quakers 1868–1929. Hicksite movement originated with the Friends' schism led by John Hicks in 1829. NRHP/HABS

FIRST FRIENDS CHURCH, E. Main and 16th streets, congregation originates from Whitewater Monthly Meeting in 1807. This monumental red brick building in a Neo-Colonial style was built in 1878 and extensively remodeled in 1926.

The presence of other religious bodies is reflected in these fine Richmond structures:

BETHEL AFRICAN METHODIST EPISCOPAL CHURCH, S. 6th and S. B streets, congregation organized in 1836, present red brick Romanesque Revival Church had been built by German Methodist congregation in 1854 and acquired by Bethel congregation in 1869. Church was extensively remodeled in 1892. NRHP/HABS

ST. JOHN LUTHERAN CHURCH, S. 7th and S. E streets, congregation founded in 1844, present red brick Gothic Revival church built in 1907. NRHP

REID MEMORIAL PRESBYTERIAN CHURCH, N. 11th and N. A streets, elegant limestone Gothic Revival structure erected in 1904, Psalm-singing Presbyterians formed congregation in 1830. The church is noted for its large Tiffany windows.

FIRST PRESBYTERIAN CHURCH, N. A and 10th streets, a fine Romanesque Revival sandstone building erected in 1886, congregation formed in 1837.

ST. PAUL EPISCOPAL CHURCH, N. A and N. 8th streets, a fine red brick Gothic Revival church built in 1849 and enlarged in the 1880s, parish was formed in 1838.

ST. ANDREW CATHOLIC CHURCH, S. C and S. 5th streets, congregation formed in 1846 and became the German Catholic parish after founding of St. Mary's parish for English-speaking Catholics in 1859; the Gothic Revival perma stone church designed by D. A. Bohlen was erected in 1900.

ST. MARY CATHOLIC CHURCH, N. A and N. 8th streets, imposing limestone and brick Renaissance Revival church designed by Cornelius Curtin dates from 1909, congregation was formed in 1859.

East Germantown (formerly Pershing), Jackson Township, located on U.S. 40, the National Highway, is home to the following historic churches:

🏛 ★ ZION LUTHERAN CHURCH, N. Milton Street near Queen Street, north of U.S. 40, congregation dates from 1822 and is the oldest Lutheran church in continuous existence in the state, the excellent red brick Gothic Revival church erected in 1900 is surrounded by a picturesque and well kept cemetery.

UNITED METHODIST CHURCH, King and Gay streets, south of U.S. 40, the congregation was organized in 1838 by Christian Augenstein, as the first church of the Evangelical Association in Indiana. The first annual conference of the Evangelical Association was held here in 1853. The white frame building dates from 1844 and has been much altered through renovations.

Cambridge City, Jackson Township, also on U.S. 40, just west of East Germantown, is the location of the following:

★ ST. ELIZABETH CATHOLIC CHURCH, W. Maple and N. Walnut streets, parish started in 1852, the present red brick Romanesque Revival church dates from 1880.

★ CAMBRIDGE CITY UNITED METHODIST CHURCH, Main (U.S. 40) and Jones streets, an elegant brick Victorian Gothic Revival church dating from 1910 for congregation founded in 1833.

PRESBYTERIAN CHURCH, W. Church and S. Green streets, limestone Gothic Revival structure built in 1858, congregation was started in 1832.

OUTSTANDING SITES ELSEWHERE IN WAYNE COUNTY:

🏛 ★ LEVI COFFIN HOUSE, U.S. 27 and Mill Street, Fountain City, New Garden Township, was the home of the noted anti-slavery activist. As anti-slavery Quakers, Coffin and his family moved from the slave state of North Carolina to Fountain City in 1826. There, Coffin, a leading local merchant, aimed to sell products made by free labor. His house dates from 1839 and became a station on the Underground Rail-

Levi Coffin House, Fountain City, Wayne County

road for fugitive slaves going northward. Coffin later moved to Cincinnati where, during the Civil War, he was agent for the Western Freedman's Aid Commission. The house is operated as a State Historical Site. NRHP/HABS/NHL/NT

★ UNITED METHODIST CHURCH, N. Green and Davis streets, Fountain City, New Garden Township, frame Gothic Revival structure dates from 1880, congregation started in 1815.

★ NEW GARDEN FRIENDS MEETING, New Garden Road near U.S. 27, south of Fountain City, New Garden Township. Organized in 1811, this meeting is the second oldest in state; the simple, red brick Federal style structure dates from 1858. Nearby parsonage was built in 1866 as school.

★ WILLIAMSBURG FRIENDS MEETING, U.S. 35 and N. Pleasant Street, Williamsburg, Green Township, carpenter built church with belfry built in 1900.

★ BOSTON CHURCH OF CHRIST, SR 227 and S. Salem Street, Boston, Boston Township, simple carpenter built structure dates from the nineteenth century.

★ BOSTON UNITED METHODIST CHURCH, W. Main Street (SR 122) near SR 227, Boston, Boston Township, simple red brick gable-front building dating from 1863, congregation established in 1806.

BETHEL CHRISTIAN CHURCH, SR 227, Bethel, Franklin Township, congregation organized in 1821, historical marker describes it as the state's oldest Christian congregation (the denomination) north of U.S. 40. The building is a white frame Italianate structure built in the 1890s.

★ GRACE BAPTIST CHURCH, Chapel Road and S. Abington Township Road, Washington Township, founded as Doddridge Methodist Episcopal Church in 1816; the present excellent red brick Italianate style church dates from 1876.

Northwest Region

Benton County

Benton County on the Illinois border is rich in farm land and low in population. The leading religious faiths are Catholic, United Methodist, and Christian Church or Church of Christ. The county is home to the following significant churches:

SACRED HEART CATHOLIC CHURCH, Main and N. Washington streets, Fowler, Center Township, the county seat, is a perma stone Gothic Revival church built in 1895, parish founded in 1875.

FIRST PRESBYTERIAN CHURCH, E. Sixth and S. Jackson streets, Fowler, Center Township, congregation organized in 1873, red brick Romanesque Revival building dates from 1896.

ST. JOHN THE BAPTIST CATHOLIC CHURCH, Fourth and Chestnut streets, Earl Park, Richland Township, red brick Romanesque Revival church built in 1902, parish started in 1880.

PRESBYTERIAN CHURCH, Elm and Sixth streets, Earl Park, Richland Township, red brick Gothic Revival structure built in 1911 for congregation organized in 1894.

OAK GROVE HERITAGE HOUSE, Benton and S. Justus streets, Oxford, Grove Township, former First Presbyterian Church now a commercial establishment, is housed in a fine red brick Romanesque Revival structure built in 1901 for congregation organized in 1853. NRHP

ST. PATRICK CATHOLIC CHURCH, E. Water and S. Michigan streets, Oxford, Grove Township, perma stone Gothic Revival church built in 1863, year of parish's founding.

OXFORD UNITED METHODIST CHURCH, E. Benton and S. Howard streets, Oxford, Grove Township, red brick Gothic Revival structure built in 1924, congregation organized in 1852.

OTTERBEIN UNITED METHODIST CHURCH, Oxford and Brown streets, Otterbein, Bolivar Township, congregation formed in 1858, present carpenter built structure dates from 1886.

ST. CHARLES CATHOLIC CHURCH, Timmons and Meadow streets, Otterbein, Bolivar Township, red brick Gothic Revival building dates from 1902, the year of the parish's founding.

CARROLL COUNTY

Carroll County's prominent religious groups are United Methodist, Christian Church or Church of Christ, and Presbyterian. The picturesque county seat, Delphi, Deer Creek Township, located on the Wabash River, is home to the following noteworthy churches:

★ FIRST BAPTIST CHURCH, E. Franklin and N. Indiana streets, congregation organized in 1829, red brick Gothic Revival church built in 1892.

★ CHURCH OF GOD OF DELPHI, W. Main and Illinois streets, former St. Mary Episcopal Church, Arts and Crafts style church built in 1901. Episcopal parish established in 1845.

★ ST. JOSEPH CATHOLIC CHURCH, W. Monroe and Washington streets, a red brick Gothic Revival structure built in 1860, year of parish founding.

FIRST PRESBYTERIAN CHURCH, E. Main and S. Indiana streets, congregation organized in 1828, limestone Gothic Revival structure built in 1909.

CHRISTIAN CHURCH, E. Main between Wilson and N. Indiana streets, brick Victorian Gothic building dates from around 1908, congregation formed in 1862.

OTHER CARROLL COUNTY SITES:

★ OLD BRETHREN GERMAN BAPTIST CHURCH, CR 250N west of SR 75, Jackson Township, carpenter built church dates from 1916.

★ SHARON BAPTIST CHURCH, Michigan Road (SR 29), Sharon, Carrollton Township, excellent Greek Revival building dates from 1870.

★ BURLINGTON CHURCH OF CHRIST, Michigan and 4th streets, Burlington, Burlington Township, red brick Gothic Revival edifice built in 1908, congregation organized in 1843.

★ BRINGHURST UNITED METHODIST CHURCH, Walnut Street, Bringhurst, Monroe Township, Gothic Revival church dates from 1874, year congregation was founded.

★ CUTLER UNITED PRESBYTERIAN CHURCH, CR 500S and SR 75, Cutler, Democrat Township, described as Germanic Gothic/ Romanesque Revival structure built in 1890.

JASPER COUNTY

Jasper County is a farming area whose leading religious groups are Catholic, United Methodist, and Reformed Church in America. The county is home to important religious institutions as well as fine church buildings:

🏛 ST. JOSEPH COLLEGE, U.S. 231 at Collegeville, south of Rensselaer, is a coeducational Catholic liberal arts college established in 1891 and conducted by the Catholic men's religious order, Society of the Most Precious Blood. The school had been started as St. Joseph Indian Normal School in 1888 by the Catholic Bureau of Indian Missions to train Native American boys in practical arts. When this venture proved unfeasible, the Precious Blood order took over the property for a men's college. The campus church is an imposing Romanesque Revival building completed in 1910. The old main building of the Normal School was later renamed Drexel Hall. NRHP

Rensselaer, Marion Township, the county seat, has several noteworthy churches:

TRINITY UNITED METHODIST CHURCH, Angelica and N. Cullen streets, originally established as Iroquois Mission in 1833 and thus is oldest religious organization in the county. The present red brick Gothic Revival church was built in 1889 and remodeled in 1911.

FIRST PRESBYTERIAN CHURCH, Angelica and N. Cullen streets, opposite Trinity Methodist, organized in 1847, red brick Classical Revival structure built in 1895, Morrison and Torrance architects.

ST. AUGUSTINE CATHOLIC CHURCH, W. Angelica and N. McKinley streets, stone Gothic Revival church built in 1939 though congregation dates from 1882.

Remington, Carpenter Township, in the county's southern part, is the site of these well preserved historic buildings that strongly evoke the historic religious life of a small rural town:

🏛 FOUNTAIN PARK CHAUTAUQUA, CR 1600S, .3 mile west of U.S. 231 on northside of Remington, was founded in 1895 by Robert Parker as an assembly for interdenominational Protestant preaching as well as lectures of prominent figures of the time. While other such Chautauqua assemblies have gone out of existence, the one at Fountain Park continues. The site includes the hotel, assembly building, and cottages built around 1900. NT

REMINGTON UNITED METHODIST CHURCH, S. Ohio and Harrison streets, congregation organized in 1870, dark brick Gothic Revival church erected in 1916.

REMINGTON PRESBYTERIAN CHURCH, S. New York and W. South streets, congregation dates from 1865, dark brick twentieth-century Classical Revival house of worship built in 1913.

SACRED HEART CATHOLIC CHURCH, N. New York and W. Michigan streets, red brick Gothic Revival structure built in 1900, parish was formed in 1875.

FIRST CHRISTIAN CHURCH, N. Ohio and Virginia streets, congregation organized in 1869, a well maintained red brick Romanesque Revival building dates from 1898.

ALSO IN JASPER COUNTY:

Former INDEPENDENCE UNITED METHODIST CHURCH, CR 500E and 375N, Gillam Township, congregation organized in 1836, simple white frame building with belfry dates from 1872, ceased to be active congregation in 1976. An extensive and well maintained cemetery surrounds building. NRHP

LAKE COUNTY

Lake County, Indiana's second most populous county after Marion County, is the home of a range of religious and ethnic groups reflecting its urban, suburban, and rural dimensions. While Catholic and Orthodox groups are prominent, the substantial African American population sustains a variety of Baptist, Methodist, and Church of God in Christ congregations. Several Lake County congregations have developed some unique buildings, such as these in the central part of the county:

🏛 ★ ST. JOHN CATHOLIC CHURCH, 93rd Ave (U.S. 41) and Wicker Avenue, St. John, St. John Township, founded in 1839 as the first congregation in Lake County. At the site is the restored original log pioneer church used by founding German immigrants, many of whom are buried in surrounding cemetery. Congregation worships in a brick Romanesque Revival structure built in 1923.

🏛 STS. CONSTANTINE and HELEN GREEK ORTHODOX CATHEDRAL and HELLENIC CULTURAL CENTER, 8000 Madison, just north of U.S. 30, Merrillville, a complex constructed in 1970–1976 for congregation formed in Gary in 1912, imposing church of modern Byzantine style seats 1,000. NT

🏛 ST. ELIJAH SERBIAN ORTHODOX CATHEDRAL, 8700 Taft Street, Merrillville, a splendid church in fourteenth-century Serbian Byzantine style, was built in 1979–1983 for parish formed in 1964, consecrated and designated cathedral in 1983—a unique modern church in a traditional architectural style.

🏛 ST. SAVA SERBIAN ORTHODOX CHURCH, Mississippi Street and 91st Street, Merrillville, is a magnificent limestone edifice in Byzantine style rising from the fields, built in 1985–1987, visible to drivers on I-65, near the U.S. 30 exit. Congregation formed in Gary in 1914 and worshipped at church located at 1300 Connecticut until destroyed by fire in 1978. The new St. Sava is a remarkable modern rendition of traditional architectural style.

The city of Gary, Lake County's largest city, is a planned corporate community founded by U.S. Steel in 1906 so that all its prominent buildings including churches were constructed in the twentieth century:

★ ST. JOHN LUTHERAN CHURCH, Taft Street and 10th Avenue, organized in 1863 by German settlers in the village of Tolleston, later annexed to Gary, thus St. John's is

Saint John Evangelist Eucharistic Adoration Chapel, near Saint John Catholic Church,
Saint John, Lake County

Saints Constantine and Helen Greek Orthodox Cathedral, Merrillville, Lake County

Saint Elijah Serbian Orthodox Cathedral, Merrillville, Lake County

the city's oldest surviving institution. Present red brick Gothic Revival church dates from 1923.

Former CITY METHODIST CHURCH, Washington Street and 6th Avenue, now an abandoned ruin but once the city's leading Methodist congregation, is a magnificent limestone Gothic complex constructed in 1925–1926. The guiding force for creating the set of buildings, Rev. William Grant Seaman, a dynamic leader in local civic and social causes, is buried in the church. The complex was the home of Indiana University extension, now Indiana University Northwest, from 1948 to 1959.

★ CHRIST EPISCOPAL CHURCH, Adams Street and 6th Avenue, not in active use as a church, a limestone Gothic building dating from 1911, parish organized in 1906.

PRIMERA IGLESIA CRISTIANA HISPAÑA, Jefferson Street and 7th Avenue, formerly Central Christian Church erected in 1923 in a brick Lombard Romanesque style with a soaring campanile, congregation formed in 1908.

★ HOLY ANGELS CATHOLIC CATHEDRAL, Tyler Street and 7th Avenue, Gothic structure with large stained-glass windows, built in 1947, parish dates from 1907, and is the cathedral of the Catholic diocese of Gary, whose jurisdiction includes northwestern Indiana.

CROSSROADS MISSIONARY BAPTIST CHURCH, 529 Jefferson Street, formerly Central Baptist Church, Gary's historic Baptist congregation, twentieth-century Classical Revival building dates from 1912.

FIRST PRESBYTERIAN CHURCH, Monroe Street and 5th Avenue, red brick Gothic Revival building dating from 1913, congregation established in 1908.

★ ST. HEDWIG'S CATHOLIC CHURCH, Connecticut Street and 17th Avenue, founded in 1908 as city's first Polish ethnic congregation, a light brick structure built in a Romanesque Revival style in 1940.

ST. CASIMIR CATHOLIC CHURCH, 1309 W. Lincoln Street, Lithuanian Catholic parish dates from 1916, a modest red brick building.

FIRST BAPTIST CHURCH, 626 W. 21st Avenue near Harrison Street, is the city's oldest black Baptist congregation founded in 1908, its pastor from 1913 to 1944, Rev. Charles Hawkins, was longtime community leader during his tenure. The church worships in a limestone Gothic revival structure.

ST. PAUL BAPTIST CHURCH, W. 23rd Avenue and Grant Street, community leader, Rev. William F. Lovelace, led this historic black church from 1926 to 1941, congregation founded in 1916, longtime location was 1938 W. Adams Street. Present church is red brick Gothic Revival structure.

KOINONIA MISSIONARY BAPTIST CHURCH, Jackson Street and W. 13th Avenue, formerly Sts. Constantine and Helen Greek Orthodox Church, built in 1912–1917, distinctive design includes dome.

MT. ZION MISSIONARY BAPTIST CHURCH, Lincoln and W. 15th Avenue, formerly St. Nicholas Carpatho-Rusin Church, a simple domed structure built in 1935.

GETHSEMANE MISSIONARY BAPTIST CHURCH, Jackson Street and 11th Avenue, originally built for Hellenic Orthodox Church, a brick Classical Revival building.

MARQUETTE PARK, Grand Boulevard and Forest Avenue, Miller, at whose entrance is a statue of Jacques Marquette, French Catholic priest and explorer, who camped at a site on the Grand Calumet River when exploring the area in 1675. His camp is believed to have been within the park grounds. The impressive statue was designed by Henry Hering of New York.

EAST CHICAGO:

ST. MARY CATHOLIC CHURCH, 144th Street and Indianapolis Boulevard, the city's first Catholic church, Gothic Revival perma stone church erected in 1916, parish dates from 1890.

ST. STANISLAUS CATHOLIC CHURCH, Maguon Avenue and 150th Street, is Polish ethnic church, built in Romanesque Revival style in 1912, parish dates from 1896.

★ ST. BASIL BYZANTINE CATHOLIC CHURCH, Indianapolis Boulevard near 143th Street, brick Byzantine style church dating from 1923.

★ APOSENTO ALTO-IGLESIA PENTECOSTAL UNIDA, Maguon Avenue and 145th Streets, former First Congregational Church, limestone twentieth-century Classical Revival building dates from 1913.

★ HOLY TRINITY CATHOLIC CHURCH, Alexander Avenue and W. 148th Street, red brick Gothic Revival church built in 1920, parish dates from 1907.

★ HOLY GHOST BYZANTINE CHURCH, 144th Street and Olcott Avenue, red brick Byzantine style church built in 1917.

★ ST. NICHOLAS ROMANIAN CATHOLIC CHURCH, Olcott Avenue and W. 143rd Street, church built in 1913 for Romanian rite Catholics.

ST. DEMETRIUS ROMANIAN BYZANTINE CATHOLIC CHURCH, 3801 Butternut Street, church erected in 1916 in brick Romanesque Revival style.

Former IMMACULATE CONCEPTION CATHOLIC CHURCH, Olcott Avenue and 149th Street, brick Romanesque Revival structure built in 1935, parish of local Italian community.

★ ST. GEORGE SERBIAN ORTHODOX CHURCH, Elm Avenue (middle of block) near 140th Street, red brick, round arched windows with onion dome, a gem erected in 1912.

ASSUMPTION CATHOLIC CHURCH, 140th Street and Elm Avenue, opposite the above, red brick Gothic Revival church for Slovak Catholics erected in 1916.

OUR LADY OF PERPETUAL HELP TRADITIONAL ROMAN CATHOLIC CHURCH, 4009 Fir Street, formerly Holy Ghost Byzantine Catholic Church, built in Byzantine style.

INDIANA HARBOR BAPTIST CHURCH, Grand and 138th streets, formerly First Baptist Church, red brick twentieth-century Gothic Revival church erected in 1928.

FIRST UNITED METHODIST CHURCH, Baring and Chicago avenues, congregation founded in 1889, red brick Gothic Revival church built in 1911.

ST. PATRICK'S CATHOLIC CHURCH, Grand Avenue and 138th streets, twentieth-century Romanesque Revival structure erected in 1922, parish organized in 1903.

WHITING:

CALUMET COLLEGE OF ST. JOSEPH, New York Avenue at 124th Street, a Catholic coeducational liberal arts college for a student body of commuters, originally a branch of St. Joseph College at Rensselaer (See Jasper County). Independent of parent institution since 1976, the college occupies former office building of Amoco Oil Company.

★ SACRED HEART CATHOLIC CHURCH, La Porte Avenue and Eighteenth Street, a massive red brick Romanesque Revival Church built in 1926–1927, is Whiting's first Catholic parish founded in 1889.

ST. JOHN THE BAPTIST CATHOLIC CHURCH, E. Benedict Street and Lincoln Avenue, monumental buff brick and limestone Romanesque Revival building dating from 1930 is the city's Slovak parish.

WHITING UNITED METHODIST CHURCH, Clark Street and Fischrupp Avenue, beautiful red brick Gothic Revival church dating from 1891, year of congregation's founding.

ST. MARY'S ASSUMPTION BYZANTINE CATHOLIC CHURCH, John Street and Clark Avenue, dark brick Byzantine style edifice built in 1918 with unique dome and spire.

HAMMOND:

★ ST. JOSEPH CATHOLIC CHURCH, Hohman Avenue and Russell Street, is an imposing presence in the heart of downtown Hammond, tan pressed brick Romanesque Revival structure built in 1912–1913, parish formed in 1897.

FIRST BAPTIST CHURCH, Sibley Street and Oakley Avenue, founded in 1888, occupying its third church building, is a huge congregation boasting 60,000 members by the 1980s. It has developed Hyles-Anderson College north of Crown Point at 8400 Burr Street.

★ ALL SAINTS CATHOLIC CHURCH, Sibley Street west of Sohl Avenue, an elegant brick Gothic Revival structure built in 1929 for congregation formed in 1896.

ST. MICHAEL THE ARCHANGEL MELKITE CATHOLIC CHURCH, Sibley Street west of Sohl Avenue, imposing brick Classical Revival structure.

★ ST. CASIMIR CATHOLIC CHURCH, S. Cameron Avenue and E. Huehn Street, brick church built in an English Gothic style in 1924, for Polish congregation formed in 1890.

"Church Row," Hohman Avenue between 165th and 173rd streets, illustrates the diversity of religious faiths in an American city. Lined up along a short stretch of Hohman Avenue, these congregations maintain buildings of modern design in a tree-lined suburban residential neighborhood. Most congregations were either established or moved to the avenue since the end of World War II and flourished through the 1950s—a period of high levels of church participation. The congregations include:

FIRST UNITED METHODIST CHURCH
FIRST UNITED LUTHERAN CHURCH
TEMPLE BETH-EL
★ ST. DEMETRIOS HELLENIC ORTHODOX CHURCH
CONGREGATION BETH ISRAEL
FIRST CHURCH OF CHRIST, SCIENTIST
TRINITY EVANGELICAL LUTHERAN CHURCH
MEADOW LANE BAPTIST CHURCH (one block east of Hohman on Meadow Lane)

HOBART:

★ FIRST UNITARIAN CHURCH, Main and 5th streets, congregation was organized in 1874, the simple brick gable-front structure with Gothic windows was completed in 1876.

★ FIRST UNITED METHODIST CHURCH, 654 E. 4th Street, an imposing twentieth-century Gothic Revival church built in 1917.

★ FIRST CHURCH OF CHRIST, SCIENTIST, 305 E. 6th Street, brick Neo-Classical style structure built in 1941.

MERRILLVILLE:

STS. PETER AND PAUL CATHOLIC CHURCH, 5885 Harrison Street, founded in 1850 when area was known as Turkey Creek, the red brick Romanesque Revival church dates from 1916.

SHRINE OF OUR LADY OF CZESTOCHOWA, 5755 Pennsylvania Street, is a Catholic shrine constructed to commemorate the 600th anniversary of the miraculous picture of the Virgin Mary at Czestochowa, Poland. Ethnic Polish priests of the Society of the Divine Savior conduct the shrine. Shrine church of contemporary design dates from 1982–1983.

SCHERERVILLE:

ST. GEORGE GREEK ORTHODOX CHURCH, W. 77th Avenue and Lincolnwood Drive, is a beautiful, modern version of traditional Byzantine-style architecture built in the 1990s for congregation formed in East Chicago in 1911.

★ ST. MICHAEL CATHOLIC CHURCH, Wilhelm and Mary streets, dates from 1874 for German settlers in area, present dark brick Romanesque Revival church built in 1930.

ELSEWHERE IN LAKE COUNTY:

★ ST. JOSEPH CATHOLIC CHURCH, Joliet (U.S. 30) and Nondorf streets, Dyer, St. John Township, is a red brick Gothic Revival church built in 1903 when area was a farming community, parish formed in 1867.

CARMELITE MONASTERY AND SHRINES, 1628 Ridge Road, Munster, is home to members of the Catholic men's religious order, the Discalced Carmelites, and on its extensive grounds visitors can find an arboretum and twenty shrines with religious sculptures.

★ FIRST UNITED METHODIST CHURCH, E. Commercial Street (SR 2) and Library Drive, Lowell, Cedar Grove Township, fine Jacobean Revival church built of brick in 1924 for congregation organized in 1870.

ST. MARY CATHOLIC CHURCH, E. Joliet at Nichols streets, Crown Point, Center Township, red brick Romanesque Revival edifice built in 1890, parish formed in 1865.

LAPORTE COUNTY

LaPorte County's leading religious groups are Catholic, United Methodist, and Lutheran Church—Missouri Synod. The county seat, LaPorte, Center Township, is home to the following group of impressive churches:

Saint George Greek Orthodox Church, Schererville, Lake County

New Church, LaPorte, LaPorte County

★ New Church (Church of the New Jerusalem), Indiana Avenue and Maple Street, congregation formed in 1842, the present Gothic Revival structure was built in 1859, unique as the only Swedenborgian church in Indiana.

★ First United Methodist Church, Michigan Avenue and Alexander Street, a splendid and imposing twentieth-century limestone Gothic church built in 1927 for city's oldest congregation dating from 1833. Its outstanding appearance brings to mind a medieval cathedral.

★ First Baptist Church, Indiana Avenue and Jefferson Street, the city's historic Baptist congregation was formed in 1838, the imposing Gothic Revival building dates from 1877.

★ St. Paul Episcopal Church, Michigan Avenue and Harrison Street, a limestone fortress in Gothic Revival style built in 1895–1898, congregation organized in 1839.

★ St. Peter Catholic Church, Michigan Avenue and Noble Street, brick Romanesque Revival structure built in 1915, parish dates from 1853.

Michigan City, Cool Spring Township, the county's major center of population, is a port community located on Lake Michigan; its historic downtown congregations represent the major faiths:

★ St. Paul Lutheran Church, Franklin and 9th streets, red brick Gothic Revival church dates from 1876, with a splendid clock tower, congregation dates from 1875 split with St. John Evangelical and Lutheran Church, founded 1856, which occupied opposite corner. St. John's former church building since 1968 has been used for commercial purposes.

★ Trinity Episcopal Church, Franklin and 6th streets, a fine limestone Romanesque Revival church built in 1880 for parish dating from 1836.

★ St. Mary of the Immaculate Conception Catholic Church, W. 10th and Buffalo streets, Gothic Revival structure built in 1868, perma stone veneer added later, parish formed in 1849.

★ St. Stanislaus Kostka Catholic Church, Washington and Ann streets, a mammoth Renaissance Revival building dating from 1926 for parish of Polish Catholics founded in 1892.

★ First Baptist Church, Spring and E. 9th streets, Neo-Classical structure built in 1914 for congregation dating from 1837.

★ First Congregational Church, Washington and 6th streets, graceful Gothic Revival building dating from 1881, congregation was organized in 1835.

★ FIRST CHRISTIAN CHURCH, Cedar and 11th streets, congregation formed in 1907, Mission style building was begun in 1925, upper church completed in 1939.

★ LINDSEY CHAPEL HOUSE OF PRAYER, Barker Avenue and York Street, founded as Swedish Memorial Scandinavian Mission Church, built in Gothic Revival style in 1910.

★ COMMUNITY CENTER OF FAITH, Buffalo and 8th streets, founded as German Methodist Church, red brick Gothic Revival structure built in 1889.

★ SACRED HEART CATHOLIC CHURCH, 8th and Kennedy streets, modest Romanesque Revival structure dating from 1916 for parish founded the previous year.

ISLAMIC CENTER OF MICHIGAN CITY, Brown Road south of U.S. 20 on city's eastside, Syrian and Lebanese immigrants formed this mosque in 1914 as the state's first Islamic congregation. The mosque on Second Street, built in the early 1920s, was reputedly the first one separately constructed in the United States. During the 1970s, the community bought the Brown Road building that was remodeled to reflect Middle Eastern appearance.

OTHER LaPORTE COUNTY SITES:

★ FIRST CHRISTIAN CHURCH, Michigan and Oak streets, Rolling Prairie, Kankakee Township, excellent Greek Revival church dating from 1859, built shortly after congregation was formed.

★ PINHOOK CEMETERY ASSOCIATION, SR 2 and Wozniak Road, New Durham Township, Greek Revival structure dating from 1847 used by Methodist and Baptist congregations, is the oldest church building in the county.

★ WESTVILLE UNITED METHODIST CHURCH, Main Street between Ridge and Clyborn streets, Westville, New Durham Township, Gothic Revival structure dates from 1867–1868, first church built in 1843.

★ ST. JOHN LUTHERAN CHURCH, CR 900W and 1550S, Cass Township, Gothic Revival structure built in 1915, nearby is the congregation's 1876 church, converted for use as a barn.

★ ST. MARTIN OF TOURS CATHOLIC CHURCH, Lowell and Dominic streets, LaCrosse, Dewey Township, Romanesque Revival church built in 1932 for congregation formed in 1860.

NEWTON COUNTY

Newton County is noted for level landscape and large farms. Its major religious groups today are Catholic, United Methodist, and American Baptist. The county has only a few substantial towns that are home to historic churches:

TRINITY UNITED METHODIST CHURCH, E. Dunlap and N. Second streets, Kentland, Jefferson Township, in the county seat, congregation organized in 1869, red brick Gothic Revival church erected in 1910.

ST. JOSEPH CATHOLIC CHURCH, 409 E. Allen Street, Kentland, Jefferson Township, red brick Romanesque Revival church erected in 1888, parish founded in 1864.

GOODLAND COMMUNITY CHURCH, N. Newton and Jasper streets, Goodland, Grant Township, formerly Griggs Memorial Methodist Church, red brick Gothic Revival structure built in 1923.

FIRST BAPTIST CHURCH, S. James and E. Union streets, Goodland, Grant Township, fine red brick Gothic Revival structure.

STS. PETER AND PAUL CATHOLIC CHURCH, Mill and S. Newton streets, Goodland, Grant Township, red brick Gothic Revival church erected in 1903, the year of parish founding.

TRINITY LUTHERAN CHURCH, U.S. 24, Goodland, Grant Township, small frame Gothic Revival church built in 1874, the year following the congregation's founding.

MT. ZION UNITED METHODIST CHURCH, 11233 S. CR 500W, near Ade, Washington Township, red brick Gothic Revival church built in 1913, congregation was started in 1867.

MOROCCO UNITED METHODIST CHURCH, Clay and Walnut streets, Morocco, Beaver Township, red brick Gothic Revival church built in 1916–1917, congregation dates from 1849.

BROOK CHRISTIAN CHURCH, S. Highway and W. Broadway streets, Brook, Iroquois Township, a well preserved red brick Romanesque Revival gem built in 1897, congregation was organized in 1895.

PORTER COUNTY

Porter County fronts on Lake Michigan, site of Indiana Dunes State Park and Indiana Dunes National Lakeshore, both of which draw large numbers of visitors to the area. The county is location of the homestead of French pioneer Joseph Bailly (NRHP/NHL/HABS). The county's leading religious groups today are Catholic, Lutheran Church—Missouri Synod, and United Methodist. The county is home to several significant religious institutions and churches representing these traditions:

🏛 VALPARAISO UNIVERSITY, Valparaiso, Center Township, is a coeducational university in the Lutheran tradition. Founded in 1859 under Methodist auspices, it later became a business institute with a large enrollment by the early twentieth century. In 1925, the Lutheran University Association, affiliated with the Lutheran Church—Missouri Synod, acquired the institution. The University is not now linked to a specific Lutheran denomination.

★ HERITAGE HALL, S. College Avenue, on the university campus, is a Victorian building dating from 1875 and is the oldest campus building. NRHP

CHAPEL OF THE RESURRECTION, is the campus place of worship, completed in 1958 according to the striking modern design of Charles Edward Stade and Associates. The chapel seats 3,000 persons for religious and university events. Nearby is campanile standing 143 feet in height with electronic carillon. NT

★ HERITAGE LUTHERAN CHURCH, N. Washington Street, Valparaiso, the county seat, founded as Immanuel Lutheran Church and given present name in 1976. This Gothic Revival church was built in 1891 for congregation founded in 1864. NRHP

OTHER SITES IN PORTER COUNTY:

★ AUGSBERG SWENSK SKOLA, E. Oak Hill Road near U.S. 12, Westchester Township, small Lutheran school serving Swedish immigrants settling in area in the 1840s, quaint gable-front structure built in 1880. HABS

★ ST. PATRICK CATHOLIC CHURCH, W. Indiana Avenue and 3rd Street, Chesterton, Westchester Township, Gothic Revival structure built in 1876, parish dates from 1858.

★ ST. PAUL EVANGELICAL LUTHERAN CHURCH, Rose Avenue and Elizabeth Street, Kouts, Pleasant Township, Gothic Revival edifice built in 1908, first church constructed in 1880.

PULASKI COUNTY

Pulaski County's major attraction to visitors is the scenic Tippecanoe River State Park. The leading religious groups present today are Catholic, United Methodist, and Christian Church or Church of Christ. Winamac, Monroe Township, the county seat, is home to these significant churches:

WINAMAC PRESBYTERIAN CHURCH, Logan and Jefferson streets, red brick Gothic Revival church built in 1889, congregation founded in 1839.

WINAMAC UNITED METHODIST CHURCH, Spring and Monticello streets, red brick Gothic Revival church built in 1900.

ST. PETER'S CATHOLIC CHURCH, Market and Madison streets, a brick Romanesque Revival church built in 1883, extensively remodeled in 1930, parish founded in 1867.

OTHER CHURCHES IN PULASKI COUNTY:

FRANCESVILLE UNITED METHODIST CHURCH, W. Montgomery and S. Salem streets, Francesville, Salem Township, red brick Gothic Revival structure built in 1904, congregation dates from 1853.

MEDARYVILLE UNITED METHODIST CHURCH, Pearl and Jefferson streets, Medaryville, White Post Township, red brick Gothic Revival church built in 1907, congregation formed in 1907.

STARKE COUNTY

Starke County is home to Bass Lake State Park and noted as the home of Henry F. Schricker, two-term Indiana governor during the 1940s. Catholic, Lutheran Church—Missouri Synod, and United Methodist are the county's major church bodies. The county, settled later than other parts of northern Indiana, has these historic church buildings:

FIRST FREE WILL BAPTIST CHURCH, E. Talmer and S. Wilson streets, Knox, Center Township, red brick Gothic Revival structure erected in 1919 for Evangelical Lutheran Church.

SAINTS CYRIL AND METHODIUS CATHOLIC CHURCH, N. Keller Street, North Judson, Wayne Township, brick Romanesque Revival structure erected in 1910, parish began in 1880.

WHITE COUNTY

White County is rich in agriculture as well as recreational opportunities on Lakes Shafer and Freeman. The major religious bodies in the county are American Baptist, United Methodist, and Catholic. The following historic congregations represent some of these traditions:

MONTICELLO UNITED METHODIST CHURCH, W. Harrison and Main streets, Monticello, Union Township, Gothic Revival stucco church built in 1887, congregation established in 1836.

★ MONON UNITED METHODIST CHURCH, Fifth and Market streets, Monon, Monon Township, red brick Romanesque Revival building erected in 1912, congregation dates from 1861.

FIRST BAPTIST CHURCH, Arch Street between 4th and 5th streets, Monon, Monon Township, brick Romanesque Revival church dates from 1907, congregation founded in 1865.

★ REYNOLDS UNITED METHODIST CHURCH, E. 2nd and Church streets, Reynolds, Honey Creek Township, red brick twentieth-century Gothic Revival structure dates from 1920.

ST. JOSEPH CATHOLIC CHURCH, SR 43 southside of Reynolds, Honey Creek Township, an imposing red brick Gothic Revival church built in 1868, parish formed in 1866.

★ ST. JAMES EVANGELICAL LUTHERAN CHURCH, N. Kenton and First streets, Reynolds, Honey Creek Township, congregation organized 1861, the fine red brick Gothic Revival building erected in 1929.

FIRST BAPTIST CHURCH, Second and Main streets, Burnettsville, Jackson Township, red brick Gothic Revival edifice, erected 1900–1904, excellent condition but the spire is missing, congregation founded in 1843.

CHURCH OF THE BRETHREN, N. Main Street, Burnettsville, Jackson Township, lovely white frame building in Gothic Revival style erected in 1890.

BETHEL CHURCH OF GOD, S. Railroad and E. Cross streets, Idaville, Jackson Township, red brick Gothic Revival building dates from 1906.

UNITED METHODIST CHURCH, S. Range (U.S. 231) and E. Anderson streets, Wolcott, Princeton Township, red brick Gothic Revival edifice dates from 1896–1903, congregation organized in 1861.

North Central Region

CASS COUNTY

Cass County's leading religious groups are United Methodist, Catholic, and Christian Church or Church of Christ. The county seat, Logansport, Eel Township, is the location of the Dentzel Carousel (NHL/NRHP) in Spencer Park. The city is also an outdoor museum of fine churches, most located along the Market and Broadway streets corridor through the city's downtown:

★ BAPTIST TEMPLE, E. Broadway and 7th streets, an imposing Classical Revival building dating from 1911, organized as Second Baptist Church in 1847.

★ FIRST UNITED METHODIST CHURCH, E. Broadway and 8th streets, formerly called Broadway United Methodist Church, a splendid Romanesque Revival monument built in 1904, congregation formed in 1830.

★ SEVENTH DAY ADVENTIST CHURCH, E. Broadway and 8th streets, a fine red brick Gothic Revival structure built in 1863 for Universalist congregation.

★ Former GRACE EVANGELICAL LUTHERAN CHURCH, E. Broadway and 9th Street, Gothic Revival stone structure built in 1870 for Presbyterian congregation.

★ FAITH UNITED METHODIST CHURCH, E. Broadway and 13th streets, a fine Neo-Classical structure dating from 1925, founded as a United Brethren congregation in 1891.

★ TRINITY EPISCOPAL CHURCH, E. Market and 7th streets, a well designed stone Gothic Revival church built in 1870, congregation was started in 1841.

★ MARKET STREET UNITED METHODIST CHURCH, E. Market and 15th streets, Romanesque Revival structure of native stone dates from 1903–1904, congregation formed in 1868.

★ CALVARY PRESBYTERIAN CHURCH, 7th and Spencer streets, an imposing limestone Gothic Revival place of worship dating from 1877 with alterations in 1893 and 1904.

★ Former ST. VINCENT DE PAUL CATHOLIC CHURCH, Spencer and 9th streets, limestone Gothic Revival building constructed in 1860–1863 for congregation formed in 1838 for Irish Catholics; the parish was merged to form All Saints Catholic Church.

ST. JAMES EVANGELICAL LUTHERAN CHURCH, 9th and Spear streets, the city's his-

Seventh Day Adventist Church, former First Universalist Church, Logansport, Cass County

(*Left to right*) Saint James Evangelical Lutheran Church, Ninth Street Christian Church, and the former Saint Vincent DePaul Church, Logansport, Cass County

toric Lutheran congregation formed in 1848, present Gothic Revival structure dates from 1867.

★ ALL SAINTS CATHOLIC CHURCH, E. Market and 2nd streets, formerly St. Joseph Catholic Church started originally for German Catholics, the Romanesque Revival church was built in 1885.

★ TRINITY LUTHERAN CHURCH, E. Market and 2nd streets, formerly St. Luke Evangelical Lutheran Church, Gothic Revival structure built in 1885 for congregation formed in 1868.

★ Former ST. BRIDGET CATHOLIC CHURCH, Wheatland Avenue and Wilkinson Street, red brick Gothic Revival church dates from 1916, parish merged to form All Saints Catholic Church.

★ CHURCH OF CHRIST, SCIENTIST, E. North and 9th streets, a fine Classical Revival building, constructed in 1913, patterned after the Christian Science Mother Church in Boston.

★ NINTH STREET CHRISTIAN CHURCH, Ninth and E. Spencer streets, an excellent Romanesque Revival building formed in 1906, congregation founded in 1842.

ELSEWHERE IN CASS COUNTY:

★ TRINITY UNITED METHODIST CHURCH, S. Chicago and South streets, Royal Center, Boone Township, interesting variation on Gothic style, structure dates from 1915, congregation founded in 1874.

★ PISGAH CHURCH, CR 600W and 50N, Jefferson Township, small Romanesque Revival church built in 1910 in picturesque rural setting with cemetery, recently faced with limestone exterior, formed as Presbyterian congregation in 1836.

★ ANOKA UNITED METHODIST CHURCH, CR 300S and 500E, Anoka, Washington Township, Late Gothic Revival church constructed in 1913, the year of congregation's founding.

★ SHILOH LUTHERAN CHURCH, Davis and E. Bishop streets, Walton, Tipton Township, red brick Gothic Revival church built in 1904 for congregation formed in 1860.

★ GALVESTON UNITED METHODIST CHURCH, E. Jackson Street, Galveston, Jackson Township, Gothic Revival structure dates from 1901, congregation started in 1853.

★ FIRST BAPTIST CHURCH, Washington and S. Sycamore streets, Galveston, Jackson Township, handsome red brick Gothic Revival church dates from 1903, congregation began in 1868.

★ CENTER UNITED METHODIST CHURCH, CR 1125S and 150E, Deer Creek Township, Neo-Classical structure built in 1914, founded as United Brethren congregation in 1885.

ELKHART COUNTY

Elkhart County has long been associated with Anabaptist Christians of the Mennonite and Amish traditions. Today's leading religious bodies in the county are Catholic, Mennonite, and Church of the Brethren. Goshen, the county seat, is home to many of the county's significant religious sites:

🏛 GOSHEN COLLEGE, College Avenue between 9th and Main streets, Goshen, is a coeducational liberal arts college conducted by the Mennonite Church. Founded at Elkhart in 1894 as Elkhart Institute of Science, Industry, and the Arts, the school was moved to Goshen in 1903 and renamed. The Mennonite Historical Library, located in the Harold and Wilma Good Library, contains literature related to the denomination and exhibits illustrating its history. NT

ASSOCIATED MENNONITE BIBLICAL SEMINARIES, 3003 Benham Avenue, is a graduate ministerial training school of the General Conference Mennonite Church operating since 1958 as a joint undertaking of Goshen Biblical Seminary (formerly on the campus of Goshen College) and Mennonite Biblical Seminary (formerly in Chicago).

★ FAITH CHRISTIAN CENTER, S. Third and Purl streets, longtime home of General Baptist Church and Shearith Israel Synagogue, the Queen Anne style building dates from 1859, with renovations in 1899.

★ FIRST UNITED METHODIST CHURCH, S. Fifth and Jefferson streets, brick Victorian Gothic church built from 1874–1877 with additions, congregation organized in 1832.

ST. JAMES EPISCOPAL CHURCH, E. Lincoln Avenue and S. Sixth Street, red brick Gothic Revival church built in 1860, parish established in 1859.

Former FIRST BAPTIST CHURCH, S. Sixth and E. Washington streets, red brick Victorian Gothic structure built in 1876 for congregation formed in 1842. Church has been used by other congregations in recent years.

FIRST PRESBYTERIAN CHURCH, E. Lincoln Avenue between Fifth and Sixth streets, congregation organized in 1853, present Gothic Revival building constructed in 1861.

FIRST UNITED CHURCH OF CHRIST, E. Lincoln Avenue and S. Fifth Street, congregation started in 1875, present small red brick Romanesque Revival church built in 1893.

OTHER SITES IN ELKHART COUNTY:

★ ST. VINCENT DE PAUL CATHOLIC CHURCH, S. Main at Prairie Street, Elkhart, Concord Township, brick Victorian Gothic church built in 1886, parish was formed in 1868.

★ ST. JOHN OF THE CROSS EPISCOPAL CHURCH, E. Vistula and Chaptoula streets, Bristol, Washington Township, Greek Revival building dates from the 1840s. NRHP

ST. JOHN LUTHERAN CHURCH, CR 15 and 32, near Goshen, Harrison Township, is a simple gable-front Greek Revival structure dating from 1853. NRHP

FULTON COUNTY

Fulton County, a region of farms and scenic lakes, is home to leading religious bodies of United Methodists, Catholics, and American Baptists. The county seat at Rochester, Rochester Township, is the location of several fine churches:

★ GRACE UNITED METHODIST CHURCH, W. Seventh and Jefferson streets, fine brick and limestone Neo-Classical structure built in 1916, congregation began in 1838.

★ TRINITY UNITED METHODIST CHURCH, W. Eighth and Jefferson streets, red brick Neo-Classical structure built in 1919, founded as Trinity Evangelical Congregation in 1878.

★ ROCHESTER CHURCH OF GOD, Pontiac and W. Sixth streets, founded as First United Brethren Church, red brick Gothic Revival structure dates from 1900.

ELSEWHERE IN FULTON COUNTY:

★ AKRON UNITED METHODIST CHURCH, N. Mishawaka and Walnut streets, Akron, Henry Township, red brick Gothic Revival structure dates from 1903–1904, congregation started in 1836.

★ FULTON BAPTIST TEMPLE, W. Dunn and Miller streets, Fulton, Liberty Township, a very imposing dark brick twentieth-century Neo-Classical church built in 1917, congregation started in 1853.

★ FLETCHER'S LAKE UNITED METHODIST CHURCH, CR 475W near 950S, Wayne Township, white carpenter built structure dates from 1896 with historic cemetery, congregation formed in 1860.

★ ST. ANN CATHOLIC CHURCH, Logan Street, Kewanna, Union Township, red brick Romanesque Revival structure built in 1919, parish dates from 1857.

HOWARD COUNTY

Howard County is home to intensive agriculture and the industrial plants of the major automobile manufacturers. The leading religious bodies are Catholic, United Methodist, and Christian Church or Church of Christ. At Kokomo, Center Township, the county seat, many congregations have left their downtown sites for newer neighborhoods, but several remain at these locations:

Former FIRST PRESBYTERIAN CHURCH, W. Walnut near Washington Street, congregation formed in 1858 and occupied this Gothic Revival church from 1889–1958, then Calvary Baptist Church used building from 1958–1989 when it was partially gutted by fire. After the fire, the facade and steeple were restored and the building was adapted for commercial uses.

GRACE UNITED METHODIST CHURCH, Washington and Mulberry streets, is the historic Methodist congregation in Kokomo organized in 1844, this mammoth Romanesque Revival church was built in 1896.

ST. PATRICK CATHOLIC CHURCH, Washington and Broadway streets, the imposing limestone Gothic Revival building with impressive stained glass windows dates from 1907, parish organized in 1858.

FIRST CONGREGATIONAL CHRISTIAN CHURCH, W. Mulberry and Webster streets, a fine twentieth-century Classical Revival church built in 1925 for congregation formed in 1863.

WAYMAN CHAPEL AFRICAN METHODIST EPISCOPAL CHURCH, N. Apperson Way and E. Havens Street, a brick and limestone Romanesque Revival structure built in 1911, congregation dates from 1873.

KOSCIUSKO COUNTY

Kosciusko County with its picturesque lakes including Indiana's largest, Lake Wawasee, has long been a Hoosier vacation and recreation mecca. The area has also attracted the interest of religious groups for summer activities. The county's leading religious bodies today are United Methodist, Catholic, and Presbyterian.

🏛 WINONA LAKE, Wayne Township, has been associated with Protestant summer activities since Rev. Solomon C. Dickey, superintendent of Home Missions of the Presbyterian Church, selected it as a location for study, educational, and entertainment activities for clergy and laity. The first annual Chautauqua Program and Bible Conference was held here in 1895 and the last in 1943. Winona Lake's halcyon years were 1900 to 1920, when many of the following buildings were constructed:

★ BILLY SUNDAY HOME, 1111 Sunday Lane, Craftsman bungalow built in 1911 for nationally famed Presbyterian evangelist and his wife who made their summer home here from 1910 until his death in 1935. His participation in Winona Lake activities was a major factor in this Christian resort's success.

HISTORICAL MARKER, Park Avenue, commemorates the life and contributions of REV. SOLOMON DICKEY (mentioned above); it stands at the site of the Sunday Tabernacle (demolished) which had been built around 1921 for Billy Sunday's meetings.

★ FIRST PRESBYTERIAN CHURCH, Chestnut and Seventh streets, formerly Winona Federated Church, Gothic Revival building dates from 1923, congregation formed in 1913.

GRACE COLLEGE AND GRACE THEOLOGICAL SEMINARY, Kingshighway and Wooster Road, is affiliated with the Fellowship of Grace Brethren Church. The seminary prepares students for ministry and has been located here since 1939; the liberal arts college was founded in 1948. Seminary and college occupy a 150-acre campus featuring attractive buildings of contemporary design.

Warsaw, Wayne Township, the county seat, located on scenic Pike Lake, has a selection of well preserved historic churches:

★ FIRST CHRISTIAN CHURCH, N. Lake and Main streets, Gothic Revival structure with sandstone veneer built in 1889, congregation founded in 1851.

★ GRACE UNITED METHODIST CHURCH, E. Market and Indiana streets, red brick Neo-Classical structure dates from 1916, congregation established in 1838.

★ ST ANNE'S EPISCOPAL CHURCH, W. Market Street, between Columbia and Pine streets, is a brick Gothic Revival structure built for Sacred Heart Catholic Church in 1876–1877. Catholic parish was formed in 1852; the Episcopal one was organized in 1861.

★ FIRST BAPTIST CHURCH, E. Center and Detroit streets, Colonial Revival structure built in 1915, congregation organized in 1851.

ELSEWHERE IN KOSCIUSKO COUNTY:

★ CAMP ALEXANDER MACK AND QUINTEN MILLER AUDITORIUM, 1100 N. Auditorium, near Milford, Van Buren Township. This Church of the Brethren Camp fronts on Lake Wabee and provides summer activities and a winter retreat in twentieth-century functional buildings dating from 1933–1940. Auditorium has remarkable mural painted by Medford D. Neher depicting history of the Church of the Brethren. NT

★ YELLOW LAKE CHURCH OF GOD CAMPGROUND, CR 900S and 675W, Seward Township, camp located on Yellow Creek Lake, dormitory built in twentieth-century functional style in 1904, with bookstore and cabins constructed in the following years.

★ FILADELFIA ASSEMBLY OF GOD, N. Harrison and E. Benton streets, Syracuse, Turkey Creek Township, was founded as Filadelfia Evangelical Church, frame Gothic Revival structure built in 1898.

★ MILFORD FIRST BRETHREN CHURCH OF CATHERINE STREET, Catherine and Henry streets, Milford, Van Buren Township, brick Gothic Revival church built in 1886 for congregation organized the previous year.

★ ETNA GREEN UNITED METHODIST CHURCH, 120 W. Broadway, Etna Green, Etna Township, Gothic Revival church built in 1915–1916, congregation started in 1865.

★ PIERCETON UNITED METHODIST CHURCH, N. 1st and Wayne streets, Pierceton, Washington Township, red brick twentieth-century Gothic Revival building constructed in 1919, congregation dates from 1854.

★ PIERCETON PRESBYTERIAN CHURCH, S. 1st Street and Church Avenue, Pierceton, Washington Township, Gothic Revival church built in 1906–1909, congregation organized in 1859.

★ MT. PLEASANT UNITED METHODIST CHURCH, CR 550S and SR 15, Clay Township, brick twentieth-century Gothic Revival church built in 1915, congregation was established in 1840.

OAKWOOD PARK, SR 13 two miles south of Syracuse, Turkey Creek Township, the much used campground of the former Evangelical Association and site of uniting session in 1951 of United Brethren conferences and Evangelical Association to form Evangelical United Brethren church.

MARSHALL COUNTY

Marshall County is noted for its scenic lakes, especially Lake Maxinkuckee, where Culver Military Academy is located. The leading religious bodies are United Methodist, Catholic, and Old Order Amish. Plymouth, Center Township, the county seat, is the location of a group of exceptionally attractive churches:

★ ST. MICHAEL CATHOLIC CHURCH, N. Center and W. Monroe streets, is an impressive brick Renaissance Revival structure built in 1910 for parish formed in 1863.

★ UNITED METHODIST CHURCH, N. Michigan and Adams streets, Neo-Classical structure built in 1914–1915, congregation was organized in 1851.

★ ST. THOMAS EPISCOPAL CHURCH, N. Center and W. Adams streets, a graceful limestone building in twentieth-century Gothic style dating from 1905–1907, the original church built in 1851 is now parish hall.

★ FIRST PRESBYTERIAN CHURCH, N. Walnut and W. Adams streets, brick Gothic Revival building painted white, constructed in 1914 for congregation organized in 1838.

FIRST UNITED CHURCH OF CHRIST, N. Center and W. Adams streets, a Romanesque Revival style building in white-painted brick, was constructed in 1869 for St. John's Evangelical and Reformed congregation, organized in 1864.

OTHER SITES IN MARSHALL COUNTY:

★ ANCILLA DOMINI COLLEGE, Union Road, south of Donaldson, West Township, a Catholic coeducational two-year college under sponsorship of the Ancilla Domini Sisters, a Catholic women's religious order. Of German origin, the Ancilla Domini Sisters arrived in Fort Wayne in 1868. In 1918 they purchased the Hotel Cecilia on Lake Gilbraith where they established their Motherhouse in a complex of buildings with Gothic style church built in 1918–1922. They opened their junior college at the site in 1937 for women and accepted men in 1967. The sisters have also been active in staffing Catholic parish schools throughout the region.

★ FIRST UNITED CHURCH OF CHRIST, S. Center and Sherman streets, Bremen, German Township, founded as German Evangelical Immanuel Church in 1856, twentieth-century Gothic Revival building dates from 1923–1924.

★ FIRST UNITED CHURCH OF CHRIST, N. Main and Liberty streets, Bourbon, Bourbon Township, Gothic Revival structure built in 1914 for First Presbyterian Church; Billy Sunday preached at cornerstone laying.

★ BOURBON UNITED METHODIST CHURCH, N. Washington and North streets, Bourbon, Bourbon Township, orange brick Gothic Revival church rebuilt in 1913, congregation dates from 1862.

★ CULVER ACADEMY MEMORIAL CHAPEL, Culver Military Academy, SR 10, Culver, Union Township, an excellent twentieth-century Gothic chapel built in 1951 as a tribute to the sixty-five hundred Culver graduates who served in World War II. Chapel and campus buildings overlook beautiful Lake Maxinkuckee.

MIAMI COUNTY

Miami County's major religious groups are United Methodist, American Baptist, and Catholic. The county seat, Peru, is famed as the birthplace of composer Cole Porter and home of Wallace Circus and American Circus Winter Quarters (NHL/NRHP), which recalls the city's prominence as headquarters of American circuses. Peru is home to these impressive historic churches located along Main Street and adjacent side streets:

CHURCH OF THE HOLY TRINITY, Main and Broadway streets, described as Anglican Catholic is Peru's historic Episcopal congregation founded in 1843. Gothic Revival brick building dates from 1914.

ST. JOHN EVANGELICAL LUTHERAN CHURCH, Main and Fremont streets, brick Gothic Revival building dates from 1875, earliest service held in 1849.

FIRST BAPTIST CHURCH, Main and Wabash streets, stone Romanesque Revival church built in 1895, congregation founded in 1866.

MAIN STREET UNITED METHODIST CHURCH, Main and Cass streets, red brick Gothic Revival edifice built in 1890, congregation formed in 1835.

FIRST PRESBYTERIAN CHURCH, Main and Cass streets, imposing limestone Gothic Revival building dates from 1905–1906, congregation founded in 1866.

ST. CHARLES BORROMEO CATHOLIC CHURCH, Cass and Fifth streets, is the county's historic Catholic parish founded in 1837, the present church was built in 1865–1867 in Gothic Revival style.

FIRST CHRISTIAN CHURCH, Main and Miami streets, a brick twentieth-century Classical Revival church built in 1916, congregation formed in 1893.

ELSEWHERE IN MIAMI COUNTY:

PAW PAW UNITED METHODIST CHURCH, Paw Paw Pike (CR 580E) near CR 800N, Richland Township, overlooks Paw Paw Creek near Eel River, congregation was organized in 1837, church erected in 1846. As one of the oldest congregations in the North Indiana Conference of the United Methodist Church, the church has been designated a United Methodist Historic Site.

BUNKER HILL UNITED METHODIST CHURCH, W. Broadway (SR 218) and N. Main streets, Bunker Hill, Deer Creek Township, red brick Gothic Revival building dates from 1901, historic congregation was organized in 1846.

FIRST BAPTIST CHURCH, W. Broadway (SR 218) and West Street, Bunker Hill, Deer Creek Township, brick twentieth-century Classical Revival building dates from 1922.

FIRST BRETHREN CHURCH, N. Main near W. Third Street, Mexico, Jefferson Township, a fine white frame Gothic Revival building unspoiled by renovations, bell visible in belfry.

CHRISTIAN CHURCH, Commerce and Columbia streets, Macy, Allen Township, large brick Romanesque Revival house of worship in excellent condition dates from 1913, congregation founded around 1868.

MACY UNITED METHODIST CHURCH, McKee and Commerce streets, Allen Township, excellent red brick Gothic Revival building dates from 1895, historic congregation began in 1842.

DENVER UNITED METHODIST CHURCH, Harrison (SR 16) and Yorick streets, Denver, Union Township, white frame Gothic Revival building with attractive belfry built in 1873, the year of congregation's founding.

DENVER BAPTIST CHURCH, Yorick Street and Washington Avenue, Denver, Union Township, white frame Gothic Revival building dates from 1887, the year after the congregation's organization.

ERIE UNITED METHODIST CHURCH, Paw Paw Pike (CR 440E) and CR 250N, Erie Township, is a very fine, small red brick Gothic Revival church built in 1900, founded as United Brethren congregation in 1849.

AMBOY FRIENDS CHURCH, E. Pennsylvania and N. Poplar streets, Amboy, Jackson Township, an elaborate red brick Romanesque Revival-Italianate building with twin towers, built in late nineteenth century for congregation formed in 1847–1848.

AMBOY UNITED METHODIST CHURCH, E. Pennsylvania and N. Poplar streets, Amboy, Jackson Township, brick Gothic Revival church built in 1913.

CHURCH OF CHRIST, E. Walnut and N. Washington streets, Converse, Jackson Township, an imposing twentieth-century Gothic Revival structure built in 1913, congregation formed in 1886.

ST. JOSEPH COUNTY

St. Joseph County, taking its name from the river flowing through it, forms with the adjacent southwestern Michigan counties the region known locally as "Michiana." In addition to recreational spots at nearby Lake Michigan, it is home to Potato Creek State Park. The county's leading religious groups are Catholic, United Methodist, and black Baptists who have left many fine buildings.

Notre Dame, on South Bend's northside, is the location of historic Catholic educational institutions associated with the men's and women's branches of the religious order, Congregation of Holy Cross:

🏛 UNIVERSITY OF NOTRE DAME, east of Michigan Street (U.S. 33) and north of Angela Boulevard, a Catholic coeducational university, was established in 1842 under leadership of French-born Rev. Edward Sorin and members of the Holy Cross order. Before Sorin's arrival, a Catholic Indian mission had been established at the site in 1832 by Rev. Stephen Badin, first Catholic priest ordained in the United States. Badin is buried in the log chapel constructed in 1906 near site of original log chapel. SACRED HEART BASILICA on campus serves as university place of worship and local parish church. The third church at the site, Sacred Heart was built in French Gothic

Sacred Heart Basilica, University of Notre Dame, Notre Dame, Saint Joseph County

style between 1871 and 1888. Its interior artistic work includes stained-glass windows from France and murals by Italian artist Luigi Gregori. The church building and its art treasures were completely restored in the 1980s. The university campus includes several historic buildings including the imposing Main Building (1879) and Sorin Hall (1889). NRHP/NT

🏛 ST. MARY'S COLLEGE, west side of N. Michigan Street (U.S. 33), one mile north of Angela Boulevard, a Catholic liberal arts college for women, was formed as St. Mary's Academy in 1855 by the Sisters of the Holy Cross and later developed a collegiate course. The campus includes the college as well as general headquarters of the Sisters of the Holy Cross whose work includes teaching in parish schools and staffing hospitals in northern Indiana and other places across the country. The principal place of worship at St. Mary's is the CHURCH OF OUR LADY OF LORETTO completed in 1886 and modeled after the Church of Santa Maria Carignano, Genoa, Italy.

HOLY CROSS COLLEGE, west side of N. Michigan Street (U.S. 33), south of St. Mary's campus and opposite the University of Notre Dame's campus, is a two-year coeducational college conducted by Brothers of Holy Cross, who opened it in 1966 in buildings of contemporary design for commuter students. Also on campus is the Provincial House of the Brothers of Holy Cross Midwest Province whose principal work historically has been staffing Catholic high schools.

South Bend, the county seat, located on the St. Joseph River, is home to the historic Studebaker home, Tippecanoe Place (NHL/NRHP) and the Old Courthouse (HABS). It is also the location of congregations representing the major faiths. The city's multi-ethnic character is reflected in several historic Catholic congregations.

DOWNTOWN CONGREGATIONS:

🏛 ST. PAUL UNITED METHODIST CHURCH, W. Colfax and Laporte avenues, was founded in 1883 as Milburn Chapel by Mrs. Clement Studebaker in memory of her father, George Milburn. The congregation was renamed St. Paul and the current building was constructed in 1901–1902 under the leadership of the Studebakers, the city's most prominent family. The Gothic Revival style church is distinguished by its fine stone work in the sanctuary and church tower; the elegant stained-glass windows were imported from Germany. The Studebakers' Tippecanoe Place is nearby on West Washington Street.

CATHEDRAL OF ST. JAMES (Episcopal), N. Lafayette Boulevard between Washington and Colfax, red brick Gothic Revival structure built in 1894, for congregation formed in 1868, official church of the bishop of the Episcopal diocese of Northern Indiana. The cathedral is noted for its Tiffany stained-glass windows. NRHP

PEOPLE'S CHURCH, Lafayette Boulevard and W. Washington Street, is a fortress-like limestone Romanesque Revival building erected in 1888 for the city's historic Presbyterian congregation formed in 1834. First Presbyterian Church is now lo-

Saint Paul United Methodist Church, South Bend, Saint Joseph County

cated in modern Neo-Colonial buildings on W. Colfax between William Street and Lafayette Blvd.

TEMPLE BETH-EL, Lafayette Boulevard and Madison Street, is the city's historic Jewish congregation formed in 1905, its current home is a building of modern design built in 1950.

FIRST UNITED METHODIST CHURCH, Madison and Main streets, congregation founded in 1831 as the city's first, the present handsome twentieth-century Gothic Revival complex was erected in 1913.

SCOTTISH RITE BUILDING, Madison and Main streets, opposite First United Methodist Church, was built in 1916 in the Classical Revival style for First Church of Christ, Scientist.

ST. PATRICK CATHOLIC CHURCH, Taylor and W. Wayne streets, buff brick Gothic Revival church built in 1887, congregation formed in 1858 and is the historic Catholic congregation in the downtown area.

ST. HEDWIG CATHOLIC CHURCH, Napier and Scott streets, buff brick Romanesque Revival church built in 1881 for the city's first Polish congregation formed in 1877.

CENTRAL UNITED METHODIST CHURCH, St. Joseph and South streets, twentieth-century Classical Revival building dating from 1927, founded as First United Brethren Church in 1910.

CHRIST TEMPLE, CHURCH OF GOD IN CHRIST, S. Michigan and Stoll streets, red brick twentieth-century Gothic Revival church built in 1922 for First Brethren congregation dating from 1886.

MARANATHA TEMPLE, S. Michigan Street, north of Sample Street, an imposing Classical Revival style building, originally built for Grace Methodist Church and then used by St. Andrew Orthodox Church from the 1950s to 1978.

EMMANUEL DELIVERANCE CHURCH OF GOD IN CHRIST, William and LaSalle streets, red brick Gothic Revival church built in 1927 for St. Peter Evangelical Church, a congregation that German immigrants formed in 1863.

ST. LUKE'S MEMORIAL CHURCH OF GOD IN CHRIST, Haney and St. Joseph streets, red brick Jacobethan Revival structure built in 1930 for Gloria Dei Lutheran Church; Swedish immigrants formed congregation in 1880.

SOUTH BEND'S HISTORIC WESTSIDE CONGREGATIONS:

ST. CASIMIR CATHOLIC CHURCH, W. Dunham and Webster streets, the city's second Polish Catholic parish founded in 1899, present church completed in 1924.

ST. STANISLAUS CATHOLIC CHURCH, N. Brookfield Street and Florence Avenue, the city's third Polish parish formed in 1898, Gothic Revival church built in 1913, limestone facing added to tower in 1954.

ST. ADALBERT CATHOLIC CHURCH, W. Huron and Olive streets, the city's fourth Polish Catholic parish, formed in 1910, massive red brick Gothic Revival church built in 1925.

ST. MARY'S POLISH NATIONAL CATHOLIC CHURCH, W. Sample and Kosciusko streets, red brick Gothic Revival building begun in 1915, this parish belongs to the independent movement of Polish Catholics.

ST. STEPHEN CATHOLIC CHURCH, W. Thomas and McPherson streets, Hungarian Catholic parish formed in 1900, present imposing brick Romanesque Revival church built in 1910.

GRACE AFRICAN METHODIST EPISCOPAL ZION CHURCH, Blaine and Vassar avenues, red brick twentieth-century Classical Revival structure built for Methodist congregation formed in 1910, occupied by present congregation since 1978.

ELIZABETH MEMORIAL CHURCH OF GOD IN CHRIST, Lincolnway West and Walnut Street, orange brick Gothic Revival structure built in 1926 for Grace Evangelical United Brethren Church.

EPWORTH UNITED METHODIST CHURCH, Lincolnway West and Olive Street, limestone twentieth-century Gothic Revival structure dates from 1912, congregation organized in 1910.

ON SOUTH BEND'S EASTSIDE:

ZION UNITED CHURCH OF CHRIST, E. Wayne and St. Peter streets, fine buff brick Gothic Revival church, built in 1888, the founding year of this historic German Evangelical congregation.

FIRST AFRICAN METHODIST EPISCOPAL ZION CHURCH, Eddy and Campeau streets, small red brick Gothic Revival church dates from 1914, rebuilt in 1924.

OLIVET AFRICAN METHODIST EPISCOPAL CHURCH, Notre Dame Avenue and Almond Street, fine red brick twentieth-century Gothic Revival church built in 1923 for Lowell Heights Methodist Church.

ST. MATTHEW CATHOLIC CATHEDRAL, Miami and Dubail streets, is the co-cathedral for the Catholic diocese of Fort Wayne-South Bend, parish organized in 1922, building of contemporary design dates from the 1950s.

CHRISTIAN CENTER CATHEDRAL OF PRAISE, 530 E. Ireland Road, is a domed house of worship in contemporary design associated with noted electronic evangelist Lester

Sumrall, now deceased. Also at site is a school (K through 12) and World Harvest Bible College, an unaccredited school of ministry.

Mishawaka, Penn Township, east of South Bend, is the county's other industrial city established on the St. Joseph River. Its churches represent the major faiths:

BETHEL COLLEGE, 1001 W. McKinley Avenue, a small coeducational liberal arts college founded in 1947 and sponsored by the Missionary Church. The library is named for former Indiana Governor Otis Bowen and his late wife Elizabeth.

FIRST UNITED METHODIST CHURCH, Church and E. Third streets, is an excellent limestone Gothic style building constructed in 1910–1911, for city's historic Methodist congregation formed in 1835.

FIRST PRESBYTERIAN CHURCH, Lincolnway and Union Street is the city's oldest congregation organized in 1834, the present Classical Revival building was constructed in 1910.

ST. JOSEPH CATHOLIC CHURCH, Mill and Third streets, imposing buff brick Gothic Revival building dates from 1891, interior preserves nineteenth-century appearance, congregation dates from 1848.

ST. BAVO CATHOLIC CHURCH, West and Seventh streets, red brick Gothic Revival building dates from 1904, founded for Belgian Catholics.

WABASH COUNTY

Wabash County's leading religious bodies are United Methodist, Church of the Brethren, and Catholic. The county draws many visitors because of the varied recreational opportunities available at Mississinewa and Salamonie Lakes. The county seat, also named Wabash, Noble Township, possesses a rich treasure of exceptional nineteenth-century buildings in its downtown historic district including the following splendid churches:

★ WABASH CHRISTIAN CHURCH, W. Hill and N. Miami streets, an excellent brick Romanesque Revival structure built in 1864, congregation founded in 1842. NRHP

★ WABASH PRESBYTERIAN CHURCH, W. Hill and N. Miami streets, directly across from Wabash Christian, is a fine red brick Gothic Revival building dating from 1880, congregation established in 1836.

★ FIRST UNITED METHODIST CHURCH, W. Sinclair and Cass streets, Victorian Gothic building constructed in 1896 for congregation organized in 1843.

★ CHURCH OF THE NAZARENE, N. Wabash and Stitt streets, formerly Wabash Street Methodist Church, limestone Gothic Revival structure built in 1903, Methodist congregation formed in 1896.

★ FRIENDS CHURCH, Adams and Pike streets, an elegant brick Romanesque Revival structure built in 1906; congregation formed in 1848.

OTHER SITES IN WABASH COUNTY:

★ MANCHESTER COLLEGE, N. Walnut Street and College Avenue, near SR 13, northside of North Manchester, Chester Township, is a coeducational liberal arts college affiliated with the Church of the Brethren (Dunkers) since 1895. The college was founded at present site in 1889 by United Brethren Church. College Hall, the administration building, is described as Victorian Functional and was built in 1890. See also the modern Petersime Chapel, built in 1962.

★ ZION LUTHERAN CHURCH, W. Main Street, between Front and Market streets, North Manchester, Chester Township, where noted author of religious novels, Lloyd C. Douglas, served as pastor 1903–1905. The congregation, dating from 1846, built the present Victorian Gothic structure in 1887 with soaring spire.

★ LOWER UNION CHURCH, CR 1300N and 400E, Chester Township, red brick Gothic Revival and Italianate style church built in 1889 with scenic location on Simontons Creek, historic cemetery at site.

★ ROANN UNITED METHODIST CHURCH, 235 Adams Street, Roann, Paw Paw Township, Gothic Revival house of worship built in 1898, congregation formed in 1866.

★ HOPEWELL CHURCH, CR 500E and 300N, Lagro Township, Gothic Revival structure built in 1872 by Methodist congregation formed in 1843. This girlhood church of Hoosier author Gene Stratton-Porter, born half mile north, now serves as community center and museum devoted to her life and works.

★ LINCOLNVILLE UNITED METHODIST CHURCH, CR 500S, south of Lincolnville, Lagro Township, brick Gothic Revival structure dates from 1915, founded as United Brethren congregation in 1854.

★ GRACE UNITED METHODIST CHURCH, Washington and Half streets, Urbana, Lagro-Paw Paw townships line, founded as Evangelical Association congregation in 1877, late Gothic Revival structure dates from 1926.

★ ST. PATRICK CATHOLIC CHURCH, Main and Harrison streets, Lagro, Lagro Township, Victorian Gothic church built in 1873, congregation formed for Irish canal workers in 1834.

WHITE'S INSTITUTE, East of SR 15 near CR 500S, north of Treaty, Noble Township, is a private secondary school operated by the Society of Friends. Founded in 1852 to teach practical skills to boys and girls on land donated by Josiah White, many students in early decades were Native Americans. Later became a technical high school, now serves needy children.

Northeast Region

Adams County

Adams County draws visitors to the Limberlost State Historic Site (NRHP) where Gene Stratton-Porter began her career as a world-renowned naturalist and author. In the nineteenth century, farming opportunities drew German immigrants to the county where they established many of today's flourishing congregations. The county's leading religious bodies are Catholic, Lutheran Church—Missouri Synod, and Old Order Amish. The historic churches in Decatur, Washington Township, the county seat, include the following:

FIRST PRESBYTERIAN CHURCH, Adams and S. 2nd streets, congregation organized in 1840, current building is a fine Gothic Revival church erected in 1902–1903.

ZION UNITED CHURCH OF CHRIST, N. 3rd and W. Jackson streets, twentieth-century Tudor Revival church built in 1923, founded as German Reformed congregation in 1863.

FIRST BAPTIST CHURCH, Jefferson and S. 2nd streets, red brick Gothic Revival structure built in 1888, congregation organized in 1850.

OTHER SITES IN ADAMS COUNTY:

SALEM UNITED CHURCH OF CHRIST, CR 600W and 750N, near Magley, Preble Township, excellent red brick Gothic Revival church built in 1892–1893, founded as German Reformed congregation in 1856.

ZION EVANGELICAL LUTHERAN CHURCH, Friedheim, CR 550W and 1050N, Preble Township, red brick Gothic Revival structure built in 1902. One of the early German Lutheran congregations in the region founded in 1838 under leadership of Lutheran pioneer Rev. Jesse Hoover. Lutheran patriarch Rev. Friedrich C. D. Wyneken was pastor from 1838–1845.

FRIEDRICH C. D. WYNEKEN HOME, CR 600W and 1000N, Preble Township, southwest of Zion Evangelical Lutheran Church, home of Lutheran patriarch during the 1860s. Plans for its restoration are under consideration.

ST. JOHN LUTHERAN CHURCH, U.S. 27 and CR 350W, Bingen, Preble Township, present Gothic Revival church built in 1877–1878; congregation of German immigrants was organized in 1845, one of the founding congregations of Lutheran Church—Missouri Synod.

Salem United Church of Christ, Preble Township, Adams County

ST. PAUL LUTHERAN CHURCH, CR 750N and 450W, Preble Township, daughter congregation of Zion Lutheran Church, Friedheim, organized in 1873, church building dates from 1883.

FIRST UNITED METHODIST CHURCH, U.S. 27 and S. Main Street, Geneva, Wabash Township, congregation organized in 1835, brick Romanesque Revival building erected in 1897.

FIRST MENNONITE CHURCH, Main and Harrison streets, Berne, Wabash Township, imposing yellow brick Tudor-Gothic Revival church erected in 1910; until the 1970s, it was the largest Mennonite congregation in the world.

ALLEN COUNTY

Allen, the state's largest county in area, includes the historic metropolis of Fort Wayne, the state's second largest city. Here the St. Joseph and St. Mary's rivers form the Maumee River. The county's leading religious groups today are Catholic, Lutheran Church—Missouri Synod, and United Methodist.

Despite urban changes, downtown Fort Wayne's historic houses of worship echo the city's nineteenth-century boast of being the "city of churches." To honor this religious heritage, the Allen County-Fort Wayne Historical Society has erected markers at important sites. These places are designated here with **ACFW**.

On the near southside of downtown Fort Wayne, these historic religious sites stand a few blocks apart:

🏛 ST. PAUL LUTHERAN CHURCH, S. Barr and E. Lewis streets, established in 1837, the congregation of one of the great founders of the Lutheran Church—Missouri Synod, Rev. Friedrich C. D. Wyneken. The present magnificent red brick Gothic Revival church was built in 1889 (NRHP/ACFW). The Indiana District Office, Lutheran Church—Missouri Synod, is located directly across from the church on Barr Street.

🏛 CATHEDRAL OF THE IMMACULATE CONCEPTION, S. Calhoun Street and Jefferson Boulevard, official church of the Catholic bishop of the diocese of Fort Wayne-South Bend. The city's first Catholic congregation was founded in the 1830s; the present Gothic Revival church dates from 1859 with Wisconsin lannonstone veneer added in the 1940s (NRHP/ACFW). Also at the site are Diocesan Chancery and the Cathedral Museum; the latter houses exhibits related to local Catholic history.

HISTORICAL MARKER, ST. MARY CATHOLIC CHURCH, Jefferson Boulevard and S. Lafayette Street, designates the site of the German Catholic congregation founded in 1848. The parish's imposing Gothic Revival church (NRHP) dating from 1886 was destroyed by fire in 1993. ACFW

The West End Historic District, just west of the downtown business area, is the site of these significant places located within an area of a few square blocks:

First Mennonite Church, Berne, Adams County

Trinity Episcopal Church, Berry and Fulton streets, an excellent Gothic Revival church built in 1865 of native sandstone, parish dates from 1839, refounded in 1843. NRHP/ACFW

Broadway Christian Church, Wayne and Broadway streets, formerly Wayne Street Methodist Episcopal Church, a congregation dating from 1849. Methodists built the imposing red brick Gothic Revival building in 1871 with extensive remodeling and additions in 1896.

Emmanuel Lutheran Church, W. Jefferson Boulevard and Union Street, congregation was formed in 1867 and built this fine red brick Gothic Revival structure.

First Presbyterian Church, Wayne at Webster streets, an imposing Neo-Colonial complex of buildings erected in 1955, replacing former church at Washington and Clinton streets. This historic congregation dates from 1831. ACFW

Plymouth United Church of Christ, Berry Street and Fairfield Avenue, founded as Plymouth Congregational Church in 1870, limestone Gothic Revival edifice built in 1923.

St. John Evangelical Lutheran Church, Washington Boulevard and Van Buren Street, a splendid Romanesque Revival structure built in 1862 and enlarged in 1928, congregation dates from 1853.

St. Paul Catholic Church, Fairfield Avenue and Washington Boulevard, red brick Romanesque Revival building dates from 1886, parish established for Germans in 1865 and now serves Hispanic Catholics.

Trinity English Lutheran Church, Wayne Street between Fairfield Avenue and Ewing Street, is a magnificent complex of limestone Gothic buildings dating from 1924, congregation formed in 1846. ACFW

Samuel Brenton House, 802 W. Wayne Street at Van Buren Street, this historic house dating from the 1850s was home to the city's pioneer Methodist clergyman, civic leader, state legislator, and antislavery member of U.S. House of Representatives during the 1850s. The brick Italianate style house was built by 1855. ACFW

Historical Marker, Fort Wayne College, 1300 W. Wayne Street and Thieme Drive, commemorates the city's historic Methodist college founded in 1846, but later moved to Upland in Grant County and renamed Taylor University, now with branch campus in Fort Wayne. ACFW

Church-related Higher Education in Fort Wayne:

🏛 Concordia Theological Seminary, 6600 Clinton Street and Martin Luther Drive, prepares candidates for ministry in the Lutheran Church—Missouri Synod. Though founded in Fort Wayne in 1846, the seminary was later moved to Missouri and

Saint Paul Lutheran Church, Fort Wayne, Allen County

Cathedral of the Immaculate Conception, Fort Wayne, Allen County

Illinois, before returning to Fort Wayne in 1977. It occupies the campus of the former Concordia Senior College, a Lutheran liberal arts college. The unique campus buildings designed by distinguished Finnish architect Eero Saarinen to resemble a North European village were built in the 1950s.

TAYLOR UNIVERSITY, FORT WAYNE CAMPUS, Rudisill Boulevard and Beaver Avenue, branch campus of the coeducational Methodist holiness institution at Upland (see East Central Region—Grant County), but founded in the city in 1846 as Fort Wayne Female College and later was named Fort Wayne College. The school was given present name in 1893 and moved to Upland. In 1992, Taylor University absorbed adjacent Summit Christian College, founded as Fort Wayne Bible College in 1895 as denominational college of the Missionary Church.

ST. FRANCIS COLLEGE, Lindenwood Avenue and Spring Street, a Catholic coeducational liberal arts college conducted by Sisters of St. Francis of Perpetual Adoration, was moved to the site in 1944 from Lafayette. The college developed around Fort Wayne magnate John H. Bass's Romanesque Revival style mansion built in 1902–1906 (NRHP). The Mansion now holds the college library.

DENOMINATIONAL OFFICES:

MISSIONARY CHURCH, INC., INTERNATIONAL OFFICES, 3901 South Wayne Avenue, is world headquarters for this denomination, which resulted from merger of the United Missionary Church and the Missionary Church Association. Many congregations can be found in northern Indiana. Bethel College at Mishawaka, Indiana is the denominational college (see North Central Region—St. Joseph County).

ELSEWHERE IN FORT WAYNE:

FIRST WAYNE STREET UNITED METHODIST CHURCH, 300 E. Wayne Street, organized in 1968, successor of two historic downtown churches, First Methodist, founded in 1830, and Wayne Street Methodist, dating from 1849. Present building was erected in a striking contemporary style in 1973 and located in the heart of downtown. ACFW

SHEPHERD OF THE CITY LUTHERAN CHURCH, 1200 Anthony Boulevard and Alliger Street, fine red brick Gothic Revival church built in 1903 for the Concordia Lutheran congregation formed in 1900.

TURNER CHAPEL AFRICAN METHODIST EPISCOPAL CHURCH, Jefferson Boulevard and Harmar Street, congregation reorganized in 1869 after earlier organization in 1845. Brick Gothic Revival church was built in 1875, remodeled in 1927. ACFW

ST. PETER CATHOLIC CHURCH, St. Martin's and Warsaw streets, is a massive red brick Gothic Revival building erected in 1893. Nearby Zion Lutheran with St. Peter's visually dominate the neighborhood once home to German immigrants. The parish, formed in 1872, gives name to St. Peter's Square Historic District.

ZION LUTHERAN CHURCH, Hanna and E. Creighton streets, a beautiful and imposing red brick Gothic Revival structure built in 1890 for congregation formed in 1883, located within view of St. Peter Catholic Church.

MOST PRECIOUS BLOOD CATHOLIC CHURCH, Barthold and Fourth streets, massive twin-spired red brick Romanesque Revival church built in 1911 for parish formed in 1889.

TRINITY LUTHERAN CHURCH, St. Mary's Avenue and Huffman Street, dark brick Gothic Revival church built in 1915 for congregation formed in 1895.

EMMAUS LUTHERAN CHURCH, Broadway Street and W. Creighton Avenue, red brick Gothic Revival church built in 1910, congregation formed in 1900.

ST. PATRICK CATHOLIC CHURCH, Harrison and Dewald streets, red brick Gothic Revival church built in 1890, year of congregation's founding.

FIRST CHURCH OF CHRIST, SCIENTIST, Fairfield and Pierce avenues, light brick Neo-Classical building dates from 1927.

FIRST BAPTIST CHURCH, Fairfield Avenue at Pierce Avenue, founded in 1837, present fine red brick and limestone Neo-Classical building dates from 1949.

ST. ANDREW CATHOLIC CHURCH, New Haven Avenue and Lumbard Street, red brick Gothic Revival building dating from 1911, parish formed in 1910.

GRACE LUTHERAN CHURCH, S. Anthony Boulevard and Colerick Street, beautiful red brick twentieth-century Gothic Revival edifice built in 1926 for congregation formed in 1891.

GRACE-ST. JOHN'S UNITED CHURCH OF CHRIST, W. Lexington Avenue and Webster Street, multicolored brick Gothic Revival building dates from 1927. Grace originated as a Reformed church in 1883 and St. John's as Reformed congregation in 1844.

PROVIDENCE BAPTIST CHURCH, Holton Avenue near E. Creighton Avenue, is a former Free Methodist church built in 1910, a small Gothic Revival building with pleasing appearance.

ACHDUTH VESHOLOM TEMPLE, Old Mill Road near Foster Park, the city's historic Jewish congregation, formerly located downtown at Wayne Street and Fairfield Avenue until the 1950s. Formed in 1848 as the Society for Visiting the Sick and Burying the Dead before taking its present name, this is the first Jewish congregation formed in the state. Historical marker downtown at W. Wayne and Harrison streets designates the temple's former location from 1859–1917. ACFW

FIRST CHRISTIAN CHURCH, 4800 S. Calhoun Street, historic Disciples of Christ congregation dates from 1871, the present Neo-Colonial style building erected in 1952.

FIRST MISSIONARY CHURCH, Rudisill Boulevard and South Wayne Street, a fine red brick Jacobean Revival building dates from 1921, congregation organized in 1905.

JOHNNY APPLESEED MEMORIAL PARK, Swanson Boulevard at Parnell Avenue, on St. Joseph River, is the site of unmarked grave of John Chapman (1774–1845), known as Johnny Appleseed, who died near Fort Wayne. This itinerant missionary spread the religious teachings of Emmanuel Swedenborg's Church of the New Jerusalem (Swedenborgian) in addition to planting apple trees. NRHP

OTHER SITES IN ALLEN COUNTY:

ST. LOUIS CATHOLIC CHURCH, 15535 E. Lincoln Highway, Besancon, Jefferson Township, Gothic Revival church built in 1870, congregation founded for French Catholics dates from 1851. The church is centerpiece of the St. Louis Besancon Historic District.

EMMANUEL LUTHERAN CHURCH, Emmanuel and Wayne Trace roads, near Exit on SR 469, Marion Township, an imposing red brick Gothic Revival structure built in 1908.

TRINITY EVANGELICAL LUTHERAN CHURCH, Decatur Road near Anthony Boulevard, Wayne Township, red brick Gothic Revival building dates from late nineteenth century.

ANTIOCH LUTHERAN CHURCH, Hoagland and Minnich roads, Marion Township, fine red brick Gothic Revival church built in 1905, congregation organized in 1855.

ST. JOSEPH CATHOLIC CHURCH, 11337 Old U.S. 27 South, Hessen Cassel, Marion Township, red brick Gothic Revival structure dates from 1857, the year of the parish's founding.

ST. ALOYSIUS CATHOLIC CHURCH, SR 1 south of Exit on SR 469, near Yoder, Pleasant Township, small red brick Romanesque Revival building, congregation formed in 1858.

ST. ROSE CATHOLIC CHURCH, Mulberry and Forest streets, Monroeville, Monroe Township, red brick Gothic Revival building dates from 1888, parish established in 1868.

ST. MARK LUTHERAN CHURCH, South and Ohio Streets, Monroeville, Monroe Township, Gothic Revival building erected in 1913, congregation formed in 1864.

ROBINSON CHAPEL UNITED METHODIST CHURCH, Union Chapel and Tonkel roads,

Cedar Creek Township, splendid carpenter built country church erected in 1878 for congregation formed in 1850.

HUNTERTOWN UNITED METHODIST CHURCH, Lima Road, northside of Huntertown, Perry Township, congregation formed in 1836, red brick Gothic Revival church dates from 1899–1900.

MONSON CHAPEL UNITED METHODIST CHURCH, 11431 Lower Huntington Road near Kress Road, Lafayette Township, carpenter built Gothic Revival church dates from 1869–1870, congregation formed in 1852.

DeKalb County

DeKalb County has a rich history of agriculture and automobile manufacturing. Its major religious bodies today are Catholic, United Methodist, and Christian Church or Church of Christ. At Auburn, Union Township, the county seat and home of the famed Auburn-Cord-Duesenberg Museum (NRHP), the following historic churches can be found:

AUBURN PRESBYTERIAN CHURCH, S. Jackson and 12th streets, an impressive Gothic Revival structure dating from 1876 with appearance modernized by limestone facing in 1960, congregation formed in 1846.

Former AUBURN BAPTIST CHURCH, N. Jackson and W. Sixth streets, painted brick Romanesque Revival church built in 1852, the year of congregation's founding.

ST. MARK LUTHERAN CHURCH, S. Van Buren and W. Ninth streets, an attractive Gothic Revival building dating from 1889, congregation was organized in 1875.

CHURCH OF CHRIST, 10th and S. Jackson streets, red brick Romanesque Revival church in excellent condition.

OTHER SITES IN DeKalb COUNTY:

ZION LUTHERAN CHURCH, CR 12, a half mile west of SR 327, Fairfield Township, white frame Gothic Revival church built in 1859, congregation organized in 1851.

ST. MICHAEL CATHOLIC CHURCH, CR 427 and CR 210, Smithfield Township, red brick Romanesque Revival church built in 1920–1922, parish organized in 1880.

ST. PETER LUTHERAN CHURCH, SR 1 and CR 68, Spencerville, Spencer Township, congregation founded in 1849 as first Lutheran church in the county, present attractive red brick Gothic Revival structure built in 1887–1889.

ST. JOSEPH CATHOLIC CHURCH, Ijams and Houston streets, Garrett, Keyser Township, dark brick Italian Renaissance style structure was built in 1921 for parish dating from 1881.

GARRETT UNITED METHODIST CHURCH, 110 W. Houston Street, Garrett, Keyser Township, dark brick twentieth-century Gothic Revival church with castle-like appearance was built in 1913, congregation dates from 1875.

CEDAR CREEK CHURCH OF THE BRETHREN, 5952 CR 7 near SR 205, Keyser Township, large white frame building dates from 1885, for congregation formed in 1854, eldest of county's Churches of the Brethren.

CHRISTIAN UNION CHURCH OF THE BRETHREN, CR 7 just north of SR 8, Keyser Township, simple but impressive red brick Gothic Revival church built in 1908.

ST. MARK'S LUTHERAN CHURCH, Main and Elm streets, Butler, Wilmington Township, red brick Romanesque Revival structure built in 1901, congregation organized in 1864.

FAITH FELLOWSHIP, Main and John streets, Butler, Wilmington Township, red brick Classical Revival church built in 1885 for United Brethren congregation formed in 1882.

WATERLOO UNITED METHODIST CHURCH, W. Maple and Elm streets, Waterloo, Grant Township, founded as First United Brethren Church in 1860, the present imposing dark brick Romanesque Revival structure dates from 1912.

ST. MARK EVANGELICAL LUTHERAN CHURCH, Washington and 3rd streets, St. Joe, Concord Township, red brick Gothic Revival structure built in 1879 and rebuilt in 1905, congregation dates from 1875.

HUNTINGTON COUNTY

Huntington County is noted for agriculture and industry and offers visitors recreational opportunities at the State Recreation Areas on Huntington and Salamonie Lakes. Its major religious groups are Catholic, United Methodist, and United Church of Christ. The county seat, Huntington, is home to an array of historic religious institutions and buildings:

🏛 ★ HUNTINGTON COLLEGE, 2303 College Avenue, is a liberal arts college sponsored by the Church of the United Brethren in Christ. It began in 1850 as Hartsville College, Hartsville, Bartholomew County. It was chartered in 1897 as Central College and moved to Huntington, acquiring its present name in 1917. The Administration Building in a Victorian Romanesque style dates from 1897. Most buildings on campus are designed in a pleasing contemporary style and located around a lake.

CHURCH OF THE UNITED BRETHREN IN CHRIST, International Headquarters, Lake and Guilford streets, is housed in a modern building near the Huntington College campus.

★ ST. PETER FIRST UNITED CHURCH OF CHRIST, Etna Avenue and Henry Street, founded as German Reformed Church, splendid Victorian Gothic church built in 1859 and remodeled in 1903. NRHP

★ FIRST PRESBYTERIAN CHURCH, E. Tipton and Warren streets, red brick late Gothic Revival structure built in 1916 for congregation formed in 1843. Vice President Dan Quayle's family worshipped here.

★ DAN QUAYLE CENTER AND MUSEUM, E. Tipton and Warren streets, the former First Church of Christ, Scientist, opposite First Presbyterian Church, is a Neo-Classical building dating from 1919. Center and museum house exhibits related to life and career of Huntington native and former Vice President Dan Quayle.

★ STS. PETER AND PAUL CATHOLIC CHURCH, N. Cherry and John streets, Gothic Revival structure built in 1866 for the city's first Catholic parish dating from 1845.

★ ST. MARY CATHOLIC CHURCH, N. Jefferson Street between John and Roche, monumental Victorian Romanesque church built in 1896, for city's English-speaking Catholics. Its onetime pastor, Rev. John F. Noll, founded *Our Sunday Visitor*, a nationally circulating Catholic newspaper, in 1912 and later became bishop of Fort Wayne.

★ FIRST BAPTIST CHURCH, E. Market Street between Warren and Guilford streets, built in 1867 and renovated in 1924; city's historic Baptist congregation dates from 1841.

★ TRINITY UNITED METHODIST CHURCH, E. Market Street near Warren Street, limestone Tudor Gothic structure built in 1914 for congregation formed in 1840, city's oldest congregation.

★ BETHEL ASSEMBLY OF GOD CHURCH, E. Franklin and Guilford streets, formerly First United Brethren Church, late Gothic Revival structure built in 1904.

★ UNITED PENTECOSTAL CHURCH, E. Franklin and Guilford streets, opposite the above, is a Victorian Romanesque church built in 1905 for Central Christian congregation founded in 1845.

★ GOOD SHEPHERD CHURCH OF THE UNITED BRETHREN IN CHRIST, Hitzfield Street and Flaxmill Road, is the former St. Felix Monastery of Catholic Franciscan order, Mission style buildings were built in 1929.

★ ST. PETER EVANGELICAL LUTHERAN CHURCH, LaFontaine Street between Stephen and John streets, red brick Gothic Revival church was built in 1870, beautifully sited on hill overlooking Huntington.

★ Former CHURCH OF THE NAZARENE, Etna Avenue and Henry Street, brick Neo-

Classical structure built in 1924, located opposite St. Peter First United Church of Christ.

★ OUR SUNDAY VISITOR BUILDING, E. Park Drive between Jefferson and Warren, Spanish Colonial structure built in 1926 for the main office of this national Catholic publication, one of the leading local industries.

★ VICTORY NOLL CONVENT, 1900 W. Park Drive, headquarters of Our Lady of Victory Missionary Sisters, a Catholic women's religious order founded here during the 1920s and devoted to religious education. Their Mission style buildings were constructed between 1924 and 1936.

OTHER SITES IN HUNTINGTON COUNTY:

HISTORICAL MARKER, U.S. 24, 7 miles west of Huntington, designates the SITE OF THE FIRST INDIAN AGRICULTURE SCHOOL IN THE WEST, established by Society of Friends. In response to appeals of Chief Little Turtle, the Baltimore (Maryland) Society of Friends sent Philip Dennis to the area to start a school in 1804 to teach farming to Indian boys and domestic arts to Indian girls. The struggling school closed during the War of 1812.

★ PLEASANT CHAPEL UNITED METHODIST CHURCH, CR 1100N near 100E, Jackson Township, formerly United Brethren congregation, Victorian Romanesque church in excellent condition was built in 1910, congregation dates from 1883.

★ FIRST BRETHREN CHURCH, S. Main and Coe streets, Roanoke, Jackson Township, this late Gothic Revival church in perma stone was built in 1908.

★ CHRIST'S UNITED METHODIST CHURCH, W. Third Street between Main and Seminary streets, Roanoke, Jackson Township, buff brick Neo-Classical style structure built in 1929, congregation formed in 1863.

★ SEMINARY UNITED METHODIST CHURCH, Seminary and 3rd streets, Roanoke, Jackson Township, founded as United Brethren congregation in 1844, lovely red brick Victorian Romanesque building dates from 1902.

★ FAITH CHAPEL UNITED METHODIST CHURCH, CR 1100N near 300W, Goblesville, Clear Creek Township, founded as Goblesville United Brethren congregation in 1862, the red brick late Gothic Revival church was built in 1902.

★ HOUSE OF PRAYER, CR 700W and Bracken Road, Makin, Warren Township, is a white frame Gothic Revival church built in 1875.

★ CHRISTIAN CHURCH, Snowden Street (CR 98S) between Jefferson and Madison, Andrews, Dallas Township, was built in Eastlake style in 1880, congregation started in 1862.

★ BUCKEYE CHRISTIAN CHURCH, CR 500E and 500S, Rock Creek Township, brick Victorian Romanesque structure built around 1900, the congregation began around 1850.

★ Former EVANGELICAL ASSOCIATION CHURCH, Clark and Curry streets, Markle, Rock Creek Township, is a handsome orange brick Victorian Romanesque building dating from 1912.

MARKLE UNITED METHODIST CHURCH, W. Morse (SR 116) and Clark (SR 3) streets, Markle, Rock Creek Township, finely preserved red brick Gothic Revival structure built in 1907, congregation dates from 1862.

★ CHURCH OF CHRIST, N. Wayne and 3rd streets, Warren, Salamonie Township, is a twentieth-century Classical Revival building constructed in 1914.

★ FIRST UNITED METHODIST CHURCH, N. Main and 3rd streets, Warren, Salamonie Township, is a fine Victorian Romanesque structure built in 1896 for town's historic Methodist congregation.

★ FIRST CHRISTIAN CHURCH, N. Main and 2nd streets, Warren, Salamonie Township, this Tudor Gothic church dates from 1902 and was remodeled in 1921.

UNITED METHODIST HOME, 7th Street and Huntington Avenue (SR 5), Warren, Salamonie Township, contains modern buildings surrounding a lovely colonial style chapel.

LAGRANGE COUNTY

Lagrange County's religious adherents are overwhelming from the Anabaptist traditions of Old Order Amish or Mennonite whose religious culture gives the county its distinctive character. United Methodists are the county's leading religious body outside the Anabaptist tradition.

🏛 MENNO-HOF MENNONITE AMISH VISITORS CENTER, SR 5, south side of Shipshewana, Newbury Township, is a non-profit information center sponsored jointly by Amish-Mennonite, Conservative Mennonite, and General Conference Mennonite churches. This carefully designed state-of-the-art museum offers visitors a guided tour through exhibits that tell the story of the Anabaptist tradition as manifested in its Hutterite, Mennonite, and Amish branches. Because Amish worship in homes and Mennonites generally worship in plain, functional buildings, this museum makes these religious traditions easily accessible to non-members. Shipshewana has long attracted visitors from across the country to its famous auctions and flea markets. To answer visitors' questions about Amish and Mennonite life, local leaders organized slide lectures in the 1980s. From these modest beginnings, they developed an important museum describing local religious and cultural life.

HISTORICAL MARKER, LAGRANGE PHALANX, U.S. 20, 9 miles east of Lagrange, locates the site of the Fourier system of communal living. From 1843 to 1848, about thirty families lived by the ideals of industry, commerce, justice, and education before their experiment collapsed. The Lagrange Phalanx is a reminder that the early freethinking Fourierist settlers intended Lagrange County to be free of churches and religious influence.

The county seat, Lagrange, is home to an attractive Renaissance Revival-style courthouse (NRHP/HABSI) and nearby are these beautiful churches:

LAGRANGE FIRST UNITED METHODIST CHURCH, Mountain and Spring streets, Lagrange, Bloomfield Township, red brick Gothic Revival structure dating from 1889, congregation was formed in 1843.

PRESBYTERIAN CHURCH, Factory and High streets, Lagrange, Bloomfield Township, congregation organized in 1843, red brick Gothic Revival building dates from 1882.

NOBLE COUNTY

Noble County is noted as location of Hoosier author Gene Stratton-Porter's "Cabin in the Wildflower Woods" (NRHP), a state historic site, and Chain of Lakes State Park. The county's leading religious groups are United Methodist, Catholic, and Lutheran Church—Missouri Synod.

Kendallville, Wayne Township, is the county's largest center of population, though not the county seat, and the location of the following distinguished church buildings:

★ IMMACULATE CONCEPTION CATHOLIC CHURCH, E. Diamond and S. Oak streets, dark brick Romanesque Revival structure was built in 1922 for parish founded in 1867.

★ TRINITY UNITED METHODIST CHURCH, S. State and E. Rush streets, an excellent red brick Gothic Revival church built in 1873, congregation was organized in 1837, the city's oldest.

★ FIRST PRESBYTERIAN CHURCH, S. State and E. William streets, brick Romanesque Revival church built in 1863, congregation formed in 1848.

★ ST. JOHN LUTHERAN CHURCH, S. Oak and E. Rush streets, red brick Tudor Revival structure built in 1925, congregation organized in 1860.

★ MITCHELL STREET UNITED METHODIST CHURCH, Riley and E. Mitchell streets, this Classical Revival building dates from 1922, founded as a Methodist Protestant congregation in 1830.

OTHER SITES IN NOBLE COUNTY:

★ LIGONIER HISTORICAL MUSEUM, S. Main Street, between Fifth and Sixth streets, Ligonier, Perry Township, formerly Ahavath Shalom (Lovers of Peace) Reform Temple, Gothic Revival building dates from 1889, last services held in 1954. The temple reflects Ligonier's rather unique past as a small rural community that once had a substantial Jewish presence.

★ CHURCH OF CHRIST, S. Cavin and Wood streets, Ligonier, Perry Township, this Greek Revival building dates from 1856 with renovations in 1898, congregation organized in 1863.

★ FIRST PRESBYTERIAN CHURCH, S. Cavin Street, Ligonier, Perry Township, a fine red brick Gothic Revival church built in 1890, congregation organized in 1836.

★ THE WAY COLLEGE OF BIBLICAL RESEARCH, SR 9, Rome City, Orange Township, a complex of buildings including the Gothic Revival church built in 1910 at the former Kneipp Springs Sanatorium, a health resort owned and operated by the Catholic women's religious order, the Sisters of the Precious Blood.

★ JEFFERSON CHRISTIAN CHURCH, CR 300E and 400N, Jefferson Township, a simple Gothic Revival church constructed in 1875.

★ CALVARY REDEMPTION CENTER, CR 1000E and 500N, Allen Township, former Allen Chapel, Greek Revival structure built in 1850 for a Methodist Protestant congregation that worshipped here until 1926. Other denominations have used the building since then. Its beauty is enhanced by the surrounding historic cemetery.

★ ST. MARY OF THE ASSUMPTION CATHOLIC CHURCH, 228 N. Main Street (SR 3), Avilla, Allen Township, brick Romanesque Revival church built in 1876 and in pristine condition inside and out, parish formed in 1853.

★ IMMACULATE CONCEPTION CATHOLIC CHURCH, CR 700E and 400S, Ege, Swan Township, brick Gothic Revival building constructed in 1923, parish founded in 1863.

★ SEVENTH DAY ADVENTIST HISTORICAL MARKER, Wolf Lake Road near CR 300W, Noble Township, designates the site of Adventist School operating from 1900 to 1918.

CAMP LUTHERHAVEN, 1596 South CR 150 West, Albion, Noble Township, is a camp sponsored by the Lutheran Church—Missouri Synod in a peaceful, bucolic setting.

STEUBEN COUNTY

Steuben County in the northeast corner of Indiana is part of the state's lake region and home to beautiful Pokagon State Park. The county's leading religious groups are United Methodist, Catholic, and Christian Church or Church of Christ. The county seat, Angola, Pleasant Township, is location of several fine church buildings:

ANGOLA UNITED METHODIST CHURCH, W. Maumee and N. West streets, red brick Gothic Revival church was built in 1889–1890 and rebuilt after fire in 1948, congregation formed in 1836.

CHURCH OF CHRIST, W. Maumee and N. Darling streets, this magnificent red brick Classical Revival structure was built in 1910, congregation organized in 1869.

FIRST CONGREGATIONAL UNITED CHURCH OF CHRIST, W. Maumee and N. Superior streets, a fine stone and brick Romanesque Revival church built in 1898–1900, congregation was established in 1869.

ELSEWHERE IN STEUBEN COUNTY:

FREE CHURCH OR POWERS CHURCH, Old SR 1 (CR 800E), .4 mile north of U.S. 20, York Township, is a New England style church built in 1876. This interdenominational church is associated with the local Powers family who were responsible for restoring the building, not used as a church since the 1920s. NRHP

ORLAND CONGREGATIONAL CHURCH, SR 120, Orland, Mill Grove Township, historic congregation organized in 1836, Greek Revival building dates from 1852 with later additions.

HUDSON UNITED BRETHREN CHURCH, Main and W. Zonker streets, Hudson, Salem Township, excellent red brick Gothic Revival structure dates from 1887.

HAMILTON UNITED METHODIST CHURCH, S. Wayne and Beecher streets, fine white frame Gothic Revival church built in 1899, congregation formed in 1838.

WELLS COUNTY

Wells County's economy is based on agriculture, but visitors are drawn to the recreational opportunities at Ouabache State Park. The county's leading religious groups are United Methodist, the Swiss ethnic Apostolic Christian Church of America, and the Evangelical Lutheran Church of America. The county has a number of fine churches located in small villages and on county roads in addition to the following in the county seat, Bluffton, Harrison Township:

FIRST BAPTIST CHURCH, W. Cherry and S. Johnson streets, is an excellent red brick late nineteenth-century Romanesque Revival structure in neighborhood south of courthouse square.

FIRST UNITED CHURCH OF CHRIST, W. Cherry and S. Main streets, originally First Reformed Church, organized in 1882, present church erected in 1882 in red brick Gothic Revival style.

OTHER PLACES IN WELLS COUNTY:

BETHEL UNITED METHODIST CHURCH, CR 300S and 450E, south of Bluffton, Harrison Township, a small, graceful Romanesque Revival gem, built in 1899 for congregation dating from 1840. NRHP

APOSTOLIC CHRISTIAN CHURCH, CR 800E and 200S north of Veracruz, Harrison Township, is an unusually massive church building for a rural area. The Apostolic Christians, a small denominational body of Swiss ethnic people, settled in the area in the nineteenth century and built this brick church seating fourteen hundred people.

EMMANUEL COMMUNITY CHURCH, CR 200N and 500W, Rock Creek Township, founded as Emmanuel Reformed Church, buff brick twentieth-century Gothic Revival structure built in 1911.

ST. PAUL LUTHERAN CHURCH, CR 300N between 100W and 200W, Rock Creek Township, an attractive red brick Gothic Revival church built in 1880.

UNIONDALE UNITED METHODIST CHURCH, Main and Hendricks streets, Union Township, this twentieth-century Classical Revival edifice was built in 1916, congregation founded in 1884.

ST. MARK LUTHERAN CHURCH, N. Sugar and Hancock streets, Uniondale, Union Township, an imposing red brick Romanesque Revival building dates from 1921, congregation dates from 1883.

FIRST PRESBYTERIAN CHURCH, Jefferson (SR 1) and Lafever streets, Ossian, Jefferson Township, red brick Gothic Revival structure was built in 1901, congregation formed in 1840.

OSSIAN UNITED METHODIST CHURCH, N. Ogden and W. Mill streets, Ossian, Jefferson Township, red brick Romanesque Revival church was built in 1899.

TOCSIN UNITED METHODIST CHURCH, Main and E. North streets, Tocsin, Jefferson Township, was founded as United Brethren congregation, this dark brick Gothic Revival church was built in 1877 and rebuilt in 1915.

PONETO UNITED METHODIST CHURCH, Walnut between Meridian and Wayne

Bethel United Methodist Church, Harrison Township, Wells County

streets, Poneto, Chester Township, red brick Gothic Revival church was built in 1905, congregation formed in 1870.

WHITLEY COUNTY

Whitley County's major religious bodies are United Methodist, Catholic, Church of God General Conference, and Lutheran Church—Missouri Synod. Columbia City, Columbia Township, the county seat, is noted as the home of Thomas R. Marshall, Indiana governor (1909–1913) and Vice President of the United States (1913–1921). A group of fine church buildings can also be found there:

COLUMBIA CITY UNITED METHODIST CHURCH, Jackson and Chauncey streets, imposing Classical Revival building dating from 1910, for congregation formed in 1843.

FIRST PRESBYTERIAN CHURCH, Jackson and Chauncey streets, a fine red brick Gothic Revival church built in 1892, congregation dates from 1852. Church of Thomas Marshall and his family.

CHURCH OF THE NAZARENE, Market and Chauncey streets, adjacent to courthouse square, brick Romanesque Revival church built for United Brethren congregation in 1901–1902.

CHURCH OF THE BRETHREN, Jackson and Washington streets, red brick Gothic Revival structure was built in 1896 for Bethel Church of God.

HISTORICAL MARKER, LLOYD C. DOUGLAS BIRTHPLACE, Main and North streets, designates the birth site of the acclaimed author of historical novels about Christ's life, *Magnificent Obsession* and *The Robe*, later made into movies. Douglas (1873–1951) was son of the pastor of Columbia City's Grace Lutheran Church. The younger Douglas became a Lutheran clergyman and was pastor of Zion Lutheran Church in North Manchester.

ELSEWHERE IN WHITLEY COUNTY:

ST. CATHERINE CATHOLIC CHURCH, U.S. 9 and CR 1000S, Nix Settlement, Washington Township, red brick Gothic Revival built ca. 1905, congregation dates from 1850.

FIRST BAPTIST CHURCH, S. Main and Mulberry streets, South Whitley, Cleveland Township, twentieth-century Classic Revival structure built in 1926, congregation was established in 1878.

SOUTH WHITLEY CHURCH OF GOD, N. Maple and East Market streets, South Whitley, Cleveland Township, fine red brick Gothic Revival building of former Methodist congregation built in 1861 and rebuilt in 1891.

COLLINS UNITED METHODIST CHURCH, SR 205 and Dorland Street, Collins, Smith Township, a compact brick Gothic Revival structure built in 1914 for Fairview United Brethren Church, a congregation started in 1879.

ST. JOHN BOSCO CATHOLIC CHURCH, N. Main (U.S. 33) and Tulley streets, Churubusco, Smith Township, a brick twentieth-century Classical Revival church built in 1917.

Index of Counties